TALES AND TRADITIONS

Readings in Chinese Literature Series

新编中文课外阅读丛书

Volume 3 POEMS, MYTHS, LOVE STORIES, AND MORE
诗、神话与爱情故事

ACTFL Level: Intermediate High to Advanced Low

SECOND EDITION

YUN XIAO   YING ZHANG   CHUNCHING CHANG

萧云   张莹   张纯青

CHENG & TSUI

"Bringing Asia to the World"™

CHENG & TSUI

"Bringing Asia to the World"™

Copyright © 2017, 2009 by
Cheng & Tsui Company, Inc.

Second Edition 2017

First Edition 2009

20 19 18 17 16   1 2 3 4 5

ISBN 978-1-62291-117-2 [Second Edition]

The Library of Congress has catalogued the first edition as:

Xiao, Yun.

    Tales & traditions : for low advanced students / Yun Xiao ... [et. al].

    p. cm. — (Readings in Chinese literature series = [Xin bian Zhong wen ke wai yue du cong shu] ; vol. 3)

    Chinese and English.

    Includes index.

    ISBN 978-0-88727-682-8 (pbk.)

    1. Chinese language—Textbooks for foreign speakers—English. 2. Fables, Chinese—Adaptations. I. Xiao, Yun. II. Title: Tales and traditions. III. Series.

PL1129.E5T32 2008

495.1'86421—dc22

                  2008062320

Printed in the United States of America

Publisher
JILL CHENG

Editorial Manager
BEN SHRAGGE

Editors
RANDY TELFER with LIJIE QIN and MIKE YONG

Creative Director
CHRISTIAN SABOGAL

Interior Design
LIZ YATES

Illustrator
KATE PAPADAKI

Cover Design
ALLISON FROST

Cover Image
© BELKAG - SHUTTERSTOCK

Cheng & Tsui Company, Inc.

Phone 1-617-988-2400 / 1-800-554-1963

Fax (617) 426-3669
25 West Street
Boston, MA 02111-1213 USA
chengtsui.co

TALES
AND
TRADITIONS

CONTENTS
目录
目錄

PREFACE TO THE SECOND EDITION

Although a number of comprehensive Chinese textbooks are currently available in the United States, interesting and informative pleasure-reading materials specifically designed for Chinese learners are scarce at all levels. Learners and instructors of Chinese as a foreign language have longed for such materials, and since the AP® Chinese Language and Culture exam was first offered in 2007, the need for quality readings that familiarize students with expressions essential to understanding Chinese culture has become greater than ever.

Tales and Traditions 《新编中文课外阅读丛书》 / 《新編中文課外閱讀叢書》 was created to meet the need for supplementary reading materials for Chinese language learners. Research on foreign language acquisition has shown that extensive pleasure reading with level-appropriate books and materials is essential to attaining fluency in a foreign language. Pleasure reading not only improves students' reading skills, speed, and language proficiency, but also leads them to lifelong fluency and enjoyment of reading in the target language. This series includes stories and poems from the Chinese literary canon that are critical for cultural competence: sayings from classical philosophers, folktales, legends, excerpts from great works of literature, and more.

Volume 3 is designed for students at ACTFL's Intermediate High or Advanced Low levels of Chinese study. The five units that comprise this volume are organized by theme. Unit 1 features five classical Chinese poems, including Li Bai's famous "Missing My Hometown on a Tranquil Night" (静夜思 / 靜夜思). Unit 2 explores well-known cities and historical sites such as Dunhuang and Tibet's Potala Palace. In Unit 3 are four classic Chinese love stories, including "The Deer Looks Back" (鹿回头 / 鹿回頭). Unit 4 features four knight-errant stories, including "The Heroine Feng Wanzhen" (女英雄冯婉贞 / 女英雄馮婉貞) and "Scraping the Poisoned Bone for Treatment" (关公刮骨疗毒 / 關公刮骨療毒). Finally, Unit 5 acquaints the reader with five myths, including "Shennong Tastes Hundreds of Herbs" (神农尝百草 / 神農嘗百草). Material within each unit increases in difficulty, but students and teachers should feel comfortable reading the selections in any order.

Each reading in *Tales and Traditions* has a vocabulary list and provocative post-text questions. The texts can be used either by students on their own or by teachers for individual student reading and/or instructor-facilitated classroom reading. Using the discussion questions, teachers can engage students through comprehension checks, cross-cultural comparisons, and real-life reflections. Students may also enjoy acting out the stories (see the "Teaching Note" at the end of this preface for more information). The texts have been designed to be easy for teachers to use and to help students gain literacy and familiarity with texts and topics at the heart of Chinese culture. With this focus on reading comprehension and cultural knowledge, *Tales and Traditions* is an excellent companion for students who are preparing for the AP® Chinese Language and Culture exam and other standardized tests.

Students can review and look up unfamiliar words by using each volume's comprehensive index of vocabulary words, arranged in alphabetical order by *pinyin*. Personal names that appear in the stories are underlined for easy recognition and identification.

About the *Tales and Traditions* Series

The four volumes that comprise this series of graded readers are each tailored to a particular level of student: by ACTFL levels, Volumes 1, 2, 3, and 4 are appropriate for Intermediate Low or Intermediate Mid, Intermediate Mid or Intermediate High, Intermediate High or Advanced Low, and Advanced Low or Advanced Mid students, respectively. The texts in the series, drawn from a variety of genres and accompanied by illustrations, span the universe of Chinese literature: myths, legends, classical and popular short stories, fables, poems from the Tang dynasty, satirical and amusing essays and stories, and extracts from well-known novels are all featured.

Vocabulary words, forms of usage, idioms, expressions, sentence patterns, and phrases have been selected according to frequency of use and expository requirements. Students should focus on reading for comprehension rather than being able to recognize each and every character, though *pinyin* texts are included in the Appendix of Volume 1 for students' reference.

To adapt the stories and compile vocabulary lists, we used three sources: *Xiandai Hanyu Pinlü Cidian* (现代汉语频率词典 / 現代漢語頻率詞典) (1986), *Hanyu Shuiping Dengji Biaozhun he Dengji Dagang* (汉语水平等级标准和等级大纲 / 漢語水平等級標準和等級大綱) (1988),

and the *Far East 3000 Chinese Character Dictionary* (远东汉字三千字典 / 遠東漢字三千字典) (2003). Words and phrases used in the series were selected based on the difficulty levels A, B, and C (甲、乙、丙) in *Hanyu Shuiping Dengji Biaozhun he Dengji Dagang*. The stories gradually increase in length with increasing level, from one hundred and fifty to one thousand characters per story for Volumes 1 and 2, and from five hundred to two thousand characters per story for Volumes 3 and 4. The readings in Volumes 1 and 2 are largely composed of the one thousand five hundred most frequently used words listed in *Xiandai Hanyu Pinlü Cidian*, whereas those in Volumes 3 and 4 are drawn from the three thousand five hundred most frequently used words.

As globalization, multiculturalism, and multilingualism change the way people interact with one another around the globe, attaining high-level Chinese language proficiency has become crucial for those who seek to gain a competitive advantage in academia, business, and other areas. We hope this series of readings will help students become not only fluent readers and speakers of Chinese, but global citizens with a multicultural perspective.

What's New in the Second Edition?

Discussion questions in the new edition of *Tales and Traditions* have been revised to better prepare students for the reading comprehension questions on the AP® Exam in Chinese Language and Culture. With a new layout, the text is now easier to read. Background information on historical figures has been added where relevant.

TEACHING NOTE

For teachers and students using this book as supplementary reading for Chinese courses, we have provided questions to stimulate class discussion of the stories in both Chinese and English. Students can also be asked to retell stories in their own words when class time allows. For extra speaking practice, students may enjoy acting out the stories in small groups. Each group can select a story, write lines of dialogue, and assign roles. A special day or two can be set aside at midterm or the end of the semester for performances.

ABBREVIATIONS OF PARTS OF SPEECH

ABBREVIATION	PART OF SPEECH
adj.	Adjective
adv.	Adverb
av.	Auxiliary verb
conj.	Conjunction
expr.	Expression
mw.	Measure word
n.	Noun
np.	Noun phrase
on.	Onomatopoeic word
part.	Particle
pn.	Proper noun
v.	Verb
vc.	Verb plus complement
vo.	Verb plus object

I

Classical Chinese Poems

第一章　诗词欣赏
第一章　詩詞欣賞

第一章　詩詞欣賞
第一章　诗词欣赏

This unit introduces five classical poems written by several of the most famous Chinese poets. These poems are very popular and included in most Chinese children's books; however, you may find them quite different from the modern Chinese language you have studied so far. The phrasing and terms are condensed and succinct, and the sentence patterns differ significantly from those found in modern Chinese.

However, these poems are beautiful. With their unique melodies and vivid images, they will help you come to a greater appreciation of the Chinese language. They are also deeply associated with Chinese literature and history, and modern Chinese readings are replete with references to these poems. Therefore, it is important and necessary for intermediate and advanced learners like you to be exposed to them. To help you bridge the gap between the classical and modern styles, we have included a prose version of each poem in modern Chinese.

By learning these poems, you will not only learn new characters and vocabulary words, but also master "old" characters and vocabulary words in a new style. And most importantly, you will become acquainted with one of the most beautiful and richest of the Chinese literary genres—诗歌 / 詩歌. We hope that through reading these poems, you will come to love the language you have committed to learning even more.

1

Missing My Hometown on a Tranquil Night

静夜思
靜夜思

Jìng yè sī

（唐）李白
（唐）李白

(Táng) Lǐ Bái

Li Bai (701–762 C.E.) is considered one of the greatest poets of the Tang dynasty, as well as all of China's literary history. Raised in what is now Sichuan (四川) Province, he is best known for the imagination and vivid imagery of his poems. Over one thousand of his poems remain to this day.

床前明月光，

Chuáng qián míng yuè guāng,

疑是地上霜。

yí shì dì shàng shuāng.

举头望明月，

Jǔ tóu wàng míng yuè,

低头思故乡。

dī tóu sī gù xiāng.

《静夜思》译文 (Prose version)

夜里我床前闪着一片明亮的光，

看起来好像是一层霜。

我抬头看见窗外的月亮，知道那只是月光。

我低头沉思，想起了我那可爱的家乡。

床前明月光，

Chuáng   qián   míng   yuè   guāng,

疑是地上霜。

yí   shì   dì   shàng   shuāng.

舉頭望明月，

Jǔ   tóu   wàng   míng   yuè,

低頭思故鄉。

dī   tóu   sī   gù   xiāng.

《靜夜思》譯文 (Prose version)

夜裡我床前閃著一片明亮的光，

看起來好像是一層霜。

我擡頭看見窗外的月光，知道那只是月光。

我低頭沉思，想起了我那可愛的家鄉。

Vocabulary List

	SIMPLIFIED CHARACTERS	TRADITIONAL CHARACTERS	PINYIN	PART OF SPEECH	ENGLISH DEFINITION
1	霜	霜	*shuāng*	n.	frost
2	举头	舉頭	*jǔ tóu*	vo.	to lift one's head
3	低头	低頭	*dī tóu*	vo.	to lower one's head
4	沉思	沉思	*chénsī*	v.	to ponder
5	故乡	故鄉	*gùxiāng*	n.	hometown
6	闪	閃	*shǎn*	v.	to shine

Questions

1 To the poet, the moonlight in front of his bed looks like
A. dew.
B. frost.
C. fog.
D. glass.

2 After gazing up at the moon, the poet lowers his head and
A. makes a wish.
B. goes to bed.
C. looks at his shadow.
D. thinks about his hometown.

3 The mood of this poem can be best described as
A. joy.
B. nostalgia.
C. emptiness.
D. confusion.

1. 诗人为什么以为床前的光是霜？
    詩人為什麽以為床前的光是霜 ？

2. 诗人后来怎么知道床前的光是月光？
    詩人後來怎麽知道床前的光是月光 ？

3. From what you have learned about Chinese traditions, why do people gaze up at the moon? What does the moon, or the shape of the moon, represent? What Chinese holidays can you think of that involve this tradition?

4. From *Tales and Traditions,* Volume 1, you may know the story behind the phrase 铁杵磨成针 / 鐵杵磨成針, and how it inspired a young Li Bai, who frequently cut classes, to begin applying himself in his studies, which included the Confucian classics. What Confucian value(s) do you think this poem represents?

2

Spring Morning

春晓
春曉

Chūn xiǎo

（唐）孟浩然
（唐）孟浩然

(Táng) Mèng Hàorán

Meng Haoran (689–740 C.E.), born in present-day Hubei (湖北) Province, was a prominent Tang dynasty poet who was strongly attached to his hometown. In fact, many of his poems are about his hometown, including its history, landscape, and even legends.

春眠不觉晓，

Chūn mián bù jué xiǎo,

处处闻啼鸟。

chù chù wén tí niǎo.

夜来风雨声，

Yè lái fēng yǔ shēng,

花落知多少？

huā luò zhī duō shǎo?

SIMPLIFIED

《春晓》译文 (Prose version)

在春天的夜里睡觉，连什么时候天亮了都不知道，

早上醒来到处都听到鸟儿的叫声。

在昨天晚上的风雨中，

谁知道有多少美丽的花儿被打落了？

春眠不覺曉，

Chūn mián bù jué xiǎo,

處處聞啼鳥。

chù chù wén tí niǎo.

夜來風雨聲，

Yè lái fēng yǔ shēng,

花落知多少？

huā luò zhī duō shǎo?

《春曉》譯文 (Prose version)

在春天的夜裡睡覺，連什麼時候天亮了都不知道，

早上醒來到處聽到鳥兒的叫聲。

在昨天晚上的風雨中，

誰知道有多少美麗的花兒被打落了？

Vocabulary List

	SIMPLIFIED CHARACTERS	TRADITIONAL CHARACTERS	PINYIN	PART OF SPEECH	ENGLISH DEFINITION
1	眠	眠	*mián*	v.	to sleep
2	不觉	不覺	*bùjué*	v.	to be unaware of
3	晓	曉	*xiǎo*	n.	dawn
4	闻	聞	*wén*	v.	to hear
5	啼鸟	啼鳥	*tíniǎo*	n.	singing birds
6	风雨	風雨	*fēngyǔ*	n.	storm of wind and rain
7	打落	打落	*dǎluò*	vc.	to knock down
8	天亮	天亮	*tiānliàng*	n.	daybreak

Questions

1 The poet is awakened by the

A. morning sunlight.

B. migrating birds.

C. sound of raindrops.

D. singing birds.

2 What caused the flower petals to fall?

A. The birds on the tree branches.

B. The wind and rain.

C. The warm sunlight.

D. The change of seasons.

3 Which of the following senses does this poem about nature evoke the most?

A. Sight

B. Smell

C. Hearing

D. Touch

1. 诗人不知道的两件事情是什么？
   詩人不知道的兩件事情是什麼？

2. This poem serves as a fine example of rhyming in Tang poetry. Which lines rhyme, and which do not? Compare this pattern with the poem you learned in the previous chapter, along with any other Tang poems you have learned, to see if this pattern is consistent.

3. Meng Haoran was known as a landscape poet, often writing about human beings in nature. While this poem is focused on the beauty of nature in springtime, its language is fairly simple. What message do you think the poet is conveying about nature through such language? How might this relate to Daoism?

3

Love Seeds

相思
相思

Xiāng sī

（唐）王维
（唐）王維

(Táng) Wáng Wéi

Wang Wei (699–761 C.E.) was a talented poet, painter, calligrapher, and musician from present-day Shaanxi (陕西 / 陝西) Province. Unlike other Tang dynasty poets such as Li Bai and Meng Haoran, Wang Wei had a successful career as a government official. Many of his four hundred poems that remain today reflect his Buddhist beliefs and compassion for nature.

红豆生南国，
Hóng   dòu   shēng   nán   guó,

春来发几枝。
chūn   lái   fā   jǐ   zhī.

愿君多采撷，
Yuàn   jūn   duō   cǎi   xié,

此物最相思。
cǐ   wù   zuì   xiāng   sī.

《相思》译文 (Prose version)

美丽的红豆生长在南方，

到了春天就会抽枝发芽。

希望你能多摘一些随身带着，

因为红豆正是情思的象征。

紅豆生南國，

Hóng *dòu* *shēng* *nán* *guó,*

春來發幾枝。

chūn *lái* *fā* *jǐ* *zhī.*

願君多採擷，

Yuàn *jūn* *duō* *cǎi* *xié,*

此物最相思。

cǐ *wù* *zuì* *xiāng* *sī.*

《相思》譯文 (Prose version)
美麗的紅豆生長在南方，
到了春天就會抽枝發芽。
希望你能多摘一些隨身帶著，
因為紅豆正是情思的象徵。

Vocabulary List

	SIMPLIFIED CHARACTERS	TRADITIONAL CHARACTERS	PINYIN	PART OF SPEECH	ENGLISH DEFINITION
1	红豆	紅豆	*hóngdòu*	n.	red bean
2	生长	生長	*shēngzhǎng*	v.	to grow
3	抽枝	抽枝	*chōu zhī*	vo.	to put forth buds
4	发芽	發芽	*fā yá*	vo.	to sprout
5	摘	摘	*zhāi*	v.	to pick, to pluck
6	情思	情思	*qíngsī*	n.	fond memories, affection, thoughts of romantic love
7	象征	象徵	*xiàngzhēng*	n.	symbol, emblem

Questions

1 Where do the red beans grow?

A. The north.

B. The south.

C. The east.

D. The west.

2 When do the red beans grow?

A. The spring.

B. The summer.

C. The fall.

D. The winter.

3 This poem is addressed to

A. the poet himself.

B. a dear friend of the poet.

C. the red beans of the south.

D. Confucius, who was known as a *junzi*, or noble scholar.

1. "君"是什么意思？
"君"是什麼意思？

2. 为什么诗人希望读者多摘一些红豆？
為什麼詩人希望讀著多摘一些紅豆？

3. Like Meng Haoran, Wang Wei is known as a landscape poet, and the two men are said to have been close friends. How does this poem compare and contrast to Meng's "Spring Morning"?

4. Why do you think red beans represent fond memories and affection?

5. What symbolizes nostalgic feelings in your cultural tradition, and how is it similar to or different from red beans in Chinese culture?

4

Pitying the Farmers

悯农
憫農

Mǐn nóng

（唐）李绅
（唐）李紳

(Táng) Lǐ Shēn

Li Shen (780–840 C.E.), born in what is now Jiangsu Province, was a great poet of the middle Tang dynasty. He obtained a *jinshi* (进士 / 進士) degree (one of the highest scholarly degrees offered by the imperial civil service exams) and served as a high-ranking official for decades. Elite as he was, he demonstrated great sympathy for poor peasants, and depicts their hardships in many of his poems.

锄禾日当午，
Chú hé rì dāng wǔ,

汗滴禾下土。
hàn dī hé xià tǔ.

谁知盘中餐，
Shuí zhī pán zhōng cān,

粒粒皆辛苦？
lì lì jiē xīn kǔ?

《悯农》译文 (Prose version)

中午太阳猛烈极了，农民们还在给禾苗锄草。

他们满身的大汗，一滴一滴落在土里。

我们吃饭的时候，有谁会想到碗里一粒一粒的米饭，

都是他们辛辛苦苦地劳动得来的呢？

鋤禾日當午，

Chú　hé　rì　dāng　wǔ,

汗滴禾下土。

hàn　dī　hé　xià　tǔ.

誰知盤中餐，

Shuí　zhī　pán　zhōng　cān,

粒粒皆辛苦？

lì　lì　jiē　xīn　kǔ?

《憫農》譯文 (Prose version)

中午太陽猛烈極了，農民們還在給禾苗鋤草。

他們滿身的大汗，一滴一滴落在土裡。

我們吃飯的時候，有誰會想到碗裡一粒一粒的米飯，

都是他們辛辛苦苦地勞動得來的呢？

Vocabulary List

	SIMPLIFIED CHARACTERS	TRADITIONAL CHARACTERS	PINYIN	PART OF SPEECH	ENGLISH DEFINITION
1	锄禾	鋤禾	*chú hé*	vo.	to hoe up weeds in the fields
2	当午	當午	*dāngwǔ*	n.	noon time
3	滴	滴	*dī*	v.	to drip
4	皆	皆	*jiē*	adv.	all, each and every
5	猛烈	猛烈	*měngliè*	adj.	fierce
6	锄头	鋤頭	*chútou*	n.	hoe
7	满身	滿身	*mǎnshēn*	vo.	to have one's body covered with
8	落在	落在	*luòzài*	vc.	to fall on
9	劳动	勞動	*láodòng*	v.	to labor, to work

Questions

Who is toiling in the fields?

A. The poet.
B. The farmers.
C. A lone farmer.
D. The poet and the farmers.

What is dripping on the soil?

A. The farmer's tears.
B. The summer raindrops.
C. The poet's last drops of drinking water.
D. None of the above.

According to the poet, each grain of rice in one's bowl

A. is bitter due to the farmers' sweat.
B. tastes great thanks to the farmers' hard work.
C. is bitter due to the farmers' tears.
D. represents the farmers' hard work.

1. 中午农民在田里做什么?
   中午農民在田裡做什麼？

2. 什么东西一滴一滴落在土里?
   什麼東西一滴一滴落在土裡？

3. 我们碗里的饭是怎么来的?
   我們碗裡的飯是怎麼來的？

4. Based on what you know about Li Shen's life, what is striking about the subject of this poem and the emotions it evokes?

5. In addition to appreciating the beauty of this poem, why do you think it is important for Chinese people, as well as people around the world, to continue revisiting it to this day?

5

Visiting the Plain of Tombs*

登乐游原
登樂遊原

Dēng lè yóu yuán

（唐）李商隐
（唐）李商隱

(Táng) Lǐ Shāngyǐn

Li Shangyin (813–858 C.E.), a Tang dynasty poet originally from what is now Henan (河南) Province, grew up in an environment of social and political decline. While he earned a *jinshi* degree like Li Shen, Li Shangyin failed to achieve a high position. The setbacks and frustrations in his life can be sensed in the tone and allusions of his poems.

*This plain was situated to the south of Xi'an where the tombs of five emperors of the Han dynasty (206 B.C.E.–220 C.E.) were located.

向晚意不适，
Xiàng wǎn yì bù shì,

驱车登古原。
qū chē dēng gǔ yuán.

夕阳无限好，
Xī yáng wú xiàn hǎo,

只是近黄昏。
zhǐ shì jìn huáng hūn.

《登乐游原》译文 (Prose version)

傍晚的时候，我觉得心里很不痛快，

便驾着马车到城郊的古原去散心。

只见快要落山的太阳光辉灿烂，美丽无比，

可惜的是，这么好的景色，马上就要到
尽头了。

向晚意不適，

Xiàng wǎn yì bù shì,

驅車登古原。

qū chē dēng gǔ yuán.

夕陽無限好，

Xī yáng wú xiàn hǎo,

只是近黃昏。

zhǐ shì jìn huáng hūn.

《登樂遊原》譯文 (Prose version)

傍晚的時候，我覺得心裡很不痛快，
便駕著馬車到城郊的古原去散心。
只見快要落山的太陽光輝燦爛，美麗無比，
可惜的是，這麼好的景色，馬上就要到
盡頭了。

Vocabulary List

	SIMPLIFIED CHARACTERS	TRADITIONAL CHARACTERS	PINYIN	PART OF SPEECH	ENGLISH DEFINITION
1	意	意	*yì*	n.	mood
2	不适	不適	*bùshì*	adj.	unhappy
3	向(傍)晚	向(傍)晚	*xiàng (bàng)wǎn*	adv.	at dusk
4	驱(驾)	驅(駕)	*qū (jià)*	v.	to drive (a horse, car, cart, etc.)
5	登	登	*dēng*	v.	to mount, to climb
6	古原	古原	*gǔyuán*	n.	the plain of ancient tombs
7	夕阳	夕陽	*xīyáng*	n.	sunset, the setting sun
8	无限	無限	*wúxiàn*	adj.	boundless
9	黄昏	黃昏	*huánghūn*	n.	dusk
10	痛快	痛快	*tòngkuai*	adj.	pleasant
11	散心	散心	*sàn xīn*	vo.	to drive away cares, to relieve boredom
12	落山	落山	*luò shān*	vo.	(of the sun) to set
13	光辉	光輝	*guānghuī*	adj.	radiant, brilliant
14	灿烂	燦爛	*cànlàn*	adj.	magnificent, splendid
15	无比	無比	*wúbǐ*	adj.	unparalleled, matchless
16	可惜	可惜	*kěxī*	adv.	unfortunately
17	尽头	盡頭	*jìntóu*	n.	the end

Questions

1 The poet is likely unhappy because

A. it is dusk and the sun is setting.

B. he is going to the plain of ancient tombs.

C. it is dusk and the temperature is falling.

D. he has to take a horse-drawn carriage
   to the plain of ancient tombs.

2 Which of the following statements is not true?

A. The poet thinks the sunset is beautiful and magnificent.

B. The poet thinks it is a pity that the sunset must come to
   an end.

C. The sunset lifts the poet's spirits.

D. The sunset does not lift the poet's spirits.

3 This ambiguous poem likely uses dusk to represent

A. the decline of a dynasty that once flourished.

B. the decline of the poet's political career.

C. the imminence of the poet's own mortality.

D. All of the above.

DISCUSSION

1. 诗人为什么要去古原？
   詩人為什麼要去古原？

2. 诗人看到夕阳的时候，他还是觉得不
   痛快吗？
   詩人看到夕陽的時候，他還是覺得不
   痛快嗎？

3. In what ways does this poem reflect Li Shangyin's own life? How might the poem also reflect the historical or political climate of the time?

4. Do you think that the poet's reaction to the beautiful scenery is due to a pessimistic outlook? Why or why not?

II

Famous Places
and Historical Sites

第二章　名胜古迹
第二章　名勝古蹟

第二章 名胜古迹

第二章 名勝古蹟

For Chinese language students, it is critical to develop a thorough understanding of China itself, including its cities and sites of historical interest, which are emblematic of the diversity of Chinese culture and civilization. This unit takes you on a journey through the Middle Kingdom from east to west, with stops at key locations: the capital city of Beijing, the Great Wall, Xi'an and Dunhuang along the Silk Road, and the sacred Potala Palace in Tibet. As many historical and legendary figures associated with these places appear in stories throughout this book, we hope that this unit will help you place some of these stories on the map.

中國首都北京

中國首都北京

6

Beijing, China's Capital City

中国首都北京
中國首都北京

Zhōngguó shǒudū Běijīng

北京是中国的首都，在中国的北部。北京很大，人口很多。北京有着三千多年的历史，它有古迹7300多个，旅游景点200多个。它集中了中国的文化，最能代表中国。所以人们常常说，在北京住上一辈子，也读不完它的历史。

　　中国人只要一说起北京，就会想起天安门广场。天安门广场是北京的象征，也是世界上最大的广场。天安门前的长安街又是世界上最长、最宽的大街。北京城外的长城，也是历史上一个有名的古迹。另外，还有颐和园，天坛和故宫，它们都是中国也是世界上最有名的古迹。故宫在北京的中心，又叫紫禁城。它一共有9999个房间，是游客们最喜欢去的地方之一。故宫是在1406年开始建造的，一共建了十四年，有二十四个皇帝在这里住过。故宫体现了中国建筑的传统特点，是北京是中國的首都，在中國的北部。北京很大，人口很多。北京有著三千多年的歷史，它有古蹟7300多個，旅遊景點200多個。它集中了中國的文化，最能代表中國。所以人們常常說，在北京住上一輩子，也讀不完它的歷史。

中國人只要一說起北京，就會想起天安門廣場。天安門廣場是北京的象徵，也是世界上最大的廣場。天安門前的長安街又是世界上最長、最寬的大街。北京城外的長城，也是歷史上一個有名的古蹟。另外，還有頤和園，天壇和故宮，它們都是中國也是世界上最有名的古蹟。故宮在北京的中心，又叫紫禁城。它一共有9999個房間，是遊客們最喜歡去的地方之一。故宮是在1406年開始建造的，一共建了十四年，有二十四個皇帝在這裡住過。故宮

中国和全世界最有名的古迹之一。

1949年，北京成为新中国的首都。北京是中国的政治、经济、和文化中心。现在，北京的经济发展非常快。2008年的第二十九届夏季奥林匹克运动会就在北京举行。全世界一共有两百多个国家和地区的运动员参加了这次盛会，在奥运五环旗下大团聚。

北京奥运的开幕式极其盛大。开幕式上最引人注意的是一幅巨大的画卷，它表现了中国历史文化的起源和发展。北京奥运会的口号为"同一个世界，同一个梦想"，英文译文是 One World, One Dream。这个口号的寓意是北京的梦想连接着整个世界，连接着世界各国人民的心。奥运会的开幕式和闭幕式在国家体育场举行，这个体育场是专为2008年奥运会建立的。因为它的外形看起来像一个鸟巢，所以又叫它"鸟巢"。

體現了中國建築的傳統特點，是中國和全世界最有名的古蹟之一。

1949年，北京成為新中國的首都。北京是中國的政治、經濟、和文化中心。現在，北京的經濟發展非常快。2008年的第二十九屆夏季奧林匹克運動會就在北京舉行。全世界一共有兩百多個國家和地區的運動員參加了這次盛會，在奧運五環旗下大團聚。

北京奧運會開幕式極其盛大。開幕式上最引人注意的是一幅巨大的畫卷，它表現了中國歷史文化的起源和發展。北京奧運會的口號為“同一個世界，同一個夢想”，英文譯文是 One World, One Dream。這個口號的寓意是北京的夢想連接著整個世界，連接著世界各國人民的心。奧運會的開幕式和閉幕式在國家體育場舉行，這個體育場是專為2008年奧運會建立的。因為它的外形

这个体育场可以坐9.1万人，除了开幕式和闭幕式以外，还是田径、足球等比赛的场地。

北京奥运会的主题歌是《我和你》。它的中文歌词是："我和你，心连心，同住地球村；为梦想，千里行，相会在北京。来吧，朋友，伸出你的手。我和你，心连心，永远是一家人。"它传递了奥运会和平、友爱和团结的精神，也传递了北京奥运会亲切、温暖的气息。

北京是中国的首都，也是中国人的骄傲。中国人常说，北京是中国的根，热爱北京，就是热爱中国，热爱中国的文化。

看起來像一個鳥巢，所以又叫它“鳥巢”。這個體育場可以坐9.1萬人，除了開幕式和閉幕式以外，還是田徑、足球等比賽的場地。

北京奧運會的主題歌是《我和你》。它的中文歌詞是：“我和你，心連心，同住地球村；為夢想，千里行，相會在北京。來吧，朋友，伸出你的手。我和你，心連心，永遠是一家人。”它傳遞了奧運會和平、友愛和團結的精神，也傳遞了北京奧運會親切、溫暖的氣息。

北京是中國的首都，也是中國人的驕傲。中國人常說，北京是中國的根，熱愛北京，就是熱愛中國，熱愛中國的文化。

Vocabulary List

	SIMPLIFIED CHARACTERS	TRADITIONAL CHARACTERS	PINYIN	PART OF SPEECH	ENGLISH DEFINITION
1	古迹	古蹟	gǔjì	n.	historic site
2	景点	景點	jǐngdiǎn	n.	scenic spot
3	集中	集中	jízhōng	v.	to focus, to centralize
4	代表	代表	dàibiǎo	v.	to represent
5	一辈子	一輩子	yī bèizi	n.	all one's life
6	天安门广场	天安門廣場	Tiān'ānmén Guǎngchǎng	pn.	Tiananmen Square
7	长安街	長安街	Cháng'ān Jiē	pn.	Chang'an Avenue
8	颐和园	頤和園	Yíhéyuán	pn.	the Summer Palace
9	天坛	天壇	Tiāntán	pn.	the Temple of Heaven
10	故宫	故宮	Gùgōng	pn.	the Imperial Palace
11	紫禁城	紫禁城	Zǐjìnchéng	pn.	the Forbidden City
12	建造	建造	jiànzào	v.	to build, to construct
13	建筑	建築	jiànzhù	n.	building, architecture
14	体现	體現	tǐxiàn	v.	to embody, to reflect

	SIMPLIFIED CHARACTERS	TRADITIONAL CHARACTERS	PINYIN	PART OF SPEECH	ENGLISH DEFINITION
15	传统	傳統	chuántǒng	n.	tradition
16	珍贵	珍貴	zhēnguì	adj.	valuable, precious
17	政治	政治	zhèngzhì	n.	politics
18	经济	經濟	jīngjì	n.	economy
19	发展	發展	fāzhǎn	n./v.	development; to develop
20	奥林匹克运动会	奧林匹克運動會	Àolínpǐkè Yùndònghuì	pn.	The Olympics
21	举行	舉行	jǔxíng	v.	to take place
22	开幕式	開幕式	kāimùshì	n.	opening ceremony
23	五环旗	五環旗	wǔhuán qí	n.	five-ring flag
24	极其	極其	jíqí	adv.	extremely
25	盛大	盛大	shèngdà	adj.	grand
26	引人注意	引人注意	yǐnrén zhùyì	adj.	attractive
27	画卷	畫卷	huàjuàn	n.	picture scroll
28	表现	表現	biǎoxiàn	v.	to express
29	起源	起源	qǐyuán	n.	origin

30	口号	口號	kǒuhào	n.	slogan
31	梦想	夢想	mèngxiǎng	n.	dream
32	寓意	寓意	yùyi	n.	implied meaning, message
33	连接	連接	liánjiē	v.	to connect
34	整个	整個	zhěnggè	adj.	entire
35	体育场	體育場	tǐyùchǎng	n.	stadium
36	外形	外形	wàixíng	n.	external form, exterior
37	鸟巢	鳥巢	niǎocháo	n.	bird's nest
38	田径	田徑	tiánjìng	n.	track and field
39	主题歌	主題歌	zhǔtígē	n.	theme song
40	地球	地球	dìqiú	n.	the Earth
41	相会	相會	xiānghuì	v.	to meet
42	传递	傳遞	chuándì	v.	to convey
43	和平	和平	hépíng	n.	peace
44	团结	團結	tuánjié	v.	to unite, to rally
45	精神	精神	jīngshén	n.	spirit
46	亲切	親切	qīnqiè	adj.	cordial, kind

	SIMPLIFIED CHARACTERS	TRADITIONAL CHARACTERS	PINYIN	PART OF SPEECH	ENGLISH DEFINITION
47	气息	氣息	*qìxī*	n.	breath, flavor
48	骄傲	驕傲	*jiāo'ào*	n.	pride
49	根	根	*gēn*	n.	root

Questions

Approximately how many years of history does Beijing have?

A. Three hundred

B. Less than three thousand

C. Over three thousand

D. Three hundred thousand

Where is Chang'an Street, known as the longest, widest street in the world?

A. The Great Wall of China

B. The Summer Palace

C. The Temple of Heaven

D. Tiananmen Square

3 How many emperors have lived in the Imperial Palace over the course of history?

A. 1,406

B. 14

C. 24

D. 9,999

4 When did Beijing become the capital of the People's Republic of China?

A. 1406

B. 1949

C. 2008

D. 1911

5 The Olympic Stadium in Beijing resembles a

A. bird's nest.

B. bird's wing.

C. bird egg.

D. bird.

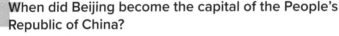
DISCUSSION

1. 为什么说北京最能代表中国？
   為什麼說北京最能代表中國？

2. 北京奥运会的主题歌的意思是什么？
   北京奧運會的主題歌的意思是什麼？

3. What makes Beijing different from other major cities in China or in other countries that you are familiar with?

4. Using resources online, research an issue that the city of Beijing is currently facing and discuss it with your class.

萬里長城
万里长城

7

The Great Wall of China

万里长城
萬里長城

Wànlǐ Chángchéng

长城是世界有名的奇迹之一，它是中国古代文化的象征和中华民族的骄傲。长城位于中国的北部，它东起河北省的山海关，西到甘肃省的嘉峪关，横贯河北、北京、内蒙古、山西、陕西、宁夏、甘肃七个省区，全长约6700公里。长城最早建于<u>秦始皇</u>时期，目的是为了防御敌人。根据历史文献记载，有20多个封建王朝先后修筑过长城，若把各个时代修筑的长城加起来，大约有10万里以上，所以中国人常常称它为"万里长城"。

八达岭长城是长城中保存得最好的一段，也是北京开放得最早的长城。它在北京的西北部，离北京市中心75公里。八达岭长城的城墙高大坚固，基部用条石筑成，有的条石有2米长，几百斤重。城墙上部由大砖砌成，地面十分平整，可以供五匹马或者十个人并列行走。八达岭城墙每隔長城是世界有名的奇蹟之一，它是中國古代文化的象徵和中華民族的驕傲。長城位於中國的北部，它東起河北省的山海關，西到甘肅省的嘉峪關，橫貫河北、北京、內蒙古、山西、陝西、寧夏、甘肅七個省區，全長約6700公里。長城最早建於秦始皇時期，目的是為了防禦敵人。根據歷史文獻記載，有20多個封建王朝先后修築過長城，若把各個時代修築的長城加起來，大約有10萬里以上，所以中國人常常稱它為"萬里長城"。

八達嶺長城是長城中保存得最好的一段，也是北京開放得最早的長城。它在北京的西北部，離北京市中心75公里。八達嶺長城的城牆高大堅固，基部用條石築成，有的條石有2米長，幾百斤重。城牆上部由大磚砌成，地面十分平整，可以供五匹馬或者十個人並列行走。

一段，就有一个堡垒式的方形城台。城台有高有低，上层可以瞭望、射击、燃放烟火，下层可以住人、休息、存放武器。在制高点上还设有烽火台，每五里到十里就有一台。遇到敌情，白天可燃烟，夜间可点火，迅速将情况报告给指挥部。

今天的长城，已不再是为了防御敌人。它成了世界有名的旅游胜地，吸引着成千上万的中外游客。至今已有包括尼克松总统，克林顿总统、撒切尔首相等三百多位世界知名人士爬过八达岭长城。

八達嶺城牆每隔一段，就有一個堡壘式的方形城台。城台有高有低，上層可以瞭望、射擊、燃放煙火，下層可以住人、休息、存放武器。在制高點上還設有烽火臺，每五里到十里就有一台。遇到敵情，白天可燃煙，夜間可點火，迅速將情況報告給指揮部。

今天的長城，已不再是為了防禦敵人。它成了世界有名的旅遊勝地，吸引著成千上萬的中外遊客。至今已有包括尼克鬆總統，克林頓總統、撒切爾首相等三百多位世界知名人士爬過八達嶺長城。

Vocabulary List

	SIMPLIFIED CHARACTERS	TRADITIONAL CHARACTERS	PINYIN	PART OF SPEECH	ENGLISH DEFINITION
1	长城	長城	*Chángchéng*	pn.	the Great Wall
2	世界	世界	*shìjiè*	n.	world
3	奇迹	奇蹟	*qíjì*	n.	miracle, wonder
4	中华民族	中華民族	*Zhōnghuá mínzú*	n.	the Chinese nationality
5	河北省	河北省	*Héběi Shěng*	pn.	Hebei Province
6	山海关	山海關	*Shānhǎi Guān*	pn.	Shanhai Pass
7	甘肃省	甘肅省	*Gānsù Shěng*	pn.	Gansu Province
8	嘉峪关	嘉峪關	*Jiāyù Guān*	pn.	Jiayu Pass
9	横贯	橫貫	*héngguàn*	v.	to cross, to traverse
10	内蒙古	內蒙古	*Nèiměnggǔ*	pn.	Inner Mongolia
11	山西	山西	*Shānxī*	pn.	Shanxi (Province)
12	陕西	陝西	*Shǎnxī*	pn.	Shaanxi (Province)
13	宁夏	寧夏	*Níngxià*	pn.	Ningxia (Autonomous Region)
14	约	約	*yuē*	adv.	approximately
15	秦始皇	秦始皇	*Qín Shǐ Huáng*	pn.	the first emperor of the Qin dynasty

	SIMPLIFIED CHARACTERS	TRADITIONAL CHARACTERS	PINYIN	PART OF SPEECH	ENGLISH DEFINITION
16	时期	時期	shíqī	n.	time period
17	目的	目的	mùdì	n.	purpose
18	防御	防禦	fángyù	v.	to guard against
19	文献	文獻	wénxiàn	n.	document
20	记载	記載	jìzǎi	n./v.	record; to record
21	封建王朝	封建王朝	fēngjiàn wángcháo	n.	feudal dynasties
22	先后	先後	xiānhòu	adv.	one after another
23	修筑	修築	xiūzhù	v.	to build, to construct
24	八达岭	八達嶺	Bādálǐng	pn.	(name of a section of the Great Wall)
25	保存	保存	bǎocún	v.	to preserve
26	坚固	堅固	jiāngù	adj.	firm, strong
27	基部	基部	jībù	n.	base
28	砌成	砌成	qìchéng	vc.	to build by laying stones
29	平整	平整	píngzhěng	adj.	neat, smooth
30	并列	並列	bìngliè	v.	to stand side by side
31	堡垒式	堡壘式	bǎolěishì	adj.	fortress-style

	SIMPLIFIED CHARACTERS	TRADITIONAL CHARACTERS	PINYIN	PART OF SPEECH	ENGLISH DEFINITION
32	方形	方形	fāngxíng	adj.	square
33	瞭望	瞭望	liàowàng	v.	to keep watch from a height or distance
34	射击	射擊	shèjī	v.	to shoot
35	燃放	燃放	ránfàng	v.	to ignite
36	烟火	煙火	yānhuǒ	n.	smoke and fire
37	存放	存放	cúnfàng	v.	to store
38	制高点	制高點	zhìgāodiǎn	n.	commanding point
39	烽火台	烽火臺	fēnghuǒtái	n.	beacon tower
40	敌情	敵情	díqíng	n.	enemy activity
41	迅速	迅速	xùnsù	adv.	quickly, swiftly
42	指挥部	指揮部	zhǐhuībù	n.	headquarters
43	旅游胜地	旅遊勝地	lǚyóu shèngdì	n.	tourist spot
44	游客	遊客	yóukè	n.	tourist
45	至今	至今	zhìjīn	adv.	so far, to this day
46	包括	包括	bāokuò	v.	to include
47	尼克松总统	尼克松總統	Níkèsōng zǒngtǒng	pn.	President Nixon

	SIMPLIFIED CHARACTERS	TRADITIONAL CHARACTERS	PINYIN	PART OF SPEECH	ENGLISH DEFINITION
48	克林顿总统	克林頓總統	*Kèlíndùn zǒngtǒng*	pn.	President Clinton
49	撒切尔首相	撒切爾首相	*Sāqiē'ěr shǒuxiàng*	pn.	Prime Minister Thatcher
50	知名人士	知名人士	*zhīmíng rénshì*	n.	public figure

Questions

1 **The Great Wall of China is located in**

A. northwestern China.

B. southern China.

C. southeastern China.

D. northern China.

2 **The Great Wall does not pass through**

A. Hubei.

B. Inner Mongolia.

C. Shaanxi.

D. Ningxia.

3 **The Great Wall of China was constructed in order to**

A. prevent citizens from fleeing.

B. guard against enemies.

C. prevent exiles from entering.

D. claim new territory.

1. 中国古代长城的作用是什么？它现在的作用
   又是什么？
   中國古代長城的作用是什麼？它現在的
   作用又是什麼？

2. 为什么中国人常常叫它"万里长城"？
   為什麼中國人常常叫它"萬里長城"？

3. Why do you think that the Great Wall of China is such a
   source of pride for Chinese people? Do you feel a sense
   of pride for a physical structure in your home country?

4. As the famous saying about the Great Wall of China goes,
   "不爬长城非好汉 / 不爬長城非好漢." What does this
   saying mean, and does it apply to you?

西安兵馬俑
西安兵马俑

8

Xi'an's Terracotta Warriors and Horses

西安兵马俑
西安兵馬俑

Xī'ān bīngmǎyǒng

西安，古时候被叫作长安，是当时中国的政治、经济、和文化中心，也是最早有一百多万人口的大城市。西安有三千多年的历史，有十多个王朝在这个城市建立都城。你如果要了解中国几千年的历史，就应该到西安去看看。"西（方）有罗马，东（方）有长安"，说的就是西安在历史上的地位跟罗马一样重要。你如果知道马可·波罗的故事，就应该知道有名的丝绸之路就是从西安开始的。如果说古埃及金字塔是世界上最大的地上王陵，那么西安的中国秦始皇陵则是世界上最大的地下皇陵。

秦始皇陵是安放秦始皇棺材的地方，它的周围有车马坑和兵马俑坑。兵马俑坑非常有名，被称为"世界第八大奇迹"。兵马俑坑又分三个坑：一号坑，二号坑，和三号坑。

安，古時候被叫作長安，是當時中國的政治、經濟、和文化中心，也是最早有一百多萬人口的大城市。西安有三千多年的歷史，有十多個王朝在這個城市建立都城。你如果要了解中國幾千年的歷史，就應該到西安去看看。"西（方）有羅馬，東（方）有長安"，說的就是西安在歷史上的地位跟羅馬一樣重要。你如果知道馬可·波羅的故事，就應該知道有名的絲綢之路就是從西安開始的。如果說古埃及金字塔是世界上最大的地上王陵，那麼西安的中國秦始皇陵則是世界上最大的地下皇陵。

秦始皇陵是安放秦始皇棺材的地方，它的周圍有車馬坑和兵馬俑坑。兵馬俑坑非常有名，被稱為"世界第八大奇蹟"。兵馬俑坑又分三個坑：一號坑，二號坑，和三號坑。

第一号兵马俑坑长230米，宽62米，面积有14260平方米。坑内有武士俑和马俑六千多件，像战场一样，排成方阵。二号坑有一千多件兵马俑，有战车和骑兵。三号坑是个小坑，好像是指挥部，它只有六十多个兵马俑。

这些兵马俑都跟真人真马一样大小，而且形态各异，表情不一。这些作品是泥塑艺术的顶峰，为中华民族的文化增添了光彩。每年都有来自世界各地的成千上万的游客去参观。

第一號兵馬俑坑長230米，寬62米，面積有14260平方米。坑內有武士俑和馬俑六千多件，像戰場一樣，排成方陣。二號坑有一千多件兵馬俑，有戰車和騎兵。三號坑是個小坑，好像是指揮部，它只有六十多個兵馬俑。

這些兵馬俑都跟真人真馬一樣大小，而且形態各異，表情不一。這些作品是泥塑藝術的頂峰，為中華民族的文化增添了光彩。每年都有來自世界各地的成千上萬的遊客去參觀。

Vocabulary List

	SIMPLIFIED CHARACTERS	TRADITIONAL CHARACTERS	PINYIN	PART OF SPEECH	ENGLISH DEFINITION
1	当时	當時	dāngshí	adv.	at that time
2	罗马	羅馬	Luómǎ	pn.	Rome
3	地位	地位	dìwèi	n.	status
4	马可·波罗	馬可·波羅	Mǎkě Bōluó	pn.	Marco Polo
5	丝绸之路	絲綢之路	Sīchóu zhī Lù	pn.	the Silk Road
6	古埃及	古埃及	Gǔ Āijí	pn.	Ancient Egypt
7	金字塔	金字塔	jīnzì tǎ	n.	pyramid
8	秦始皇陵	秦始皇陵	Qín Shǐ Huáng Líng	pn.	the tomb of Emperor Qin Shi Huang
9	棺材	棺材	guāncái	n.	coffin
10	兵马俑坑	兵馬俑坑	Bīngmǎyǒng Kēng	pn.	Vault of Warriors and Horses
11	武士俑	武士俑	wǔshìyǒng	n.	warriors
12	战场	戰場	zhànchǎng	n.	battleground
13	排成方阵	排成方陣	páichéng fāngzhèn	vo.	to line up in a square formation
14	骑兵	騎兵	qíbīng	n.	cavalrymen
15	形态	形態	xíngtài	n.	form, shape

	SIMPLIFIED CHARACTERS	TRADITIONAL CHARACTERS	PINYIN	PART OF SPEECH	ENGLISH DEFINITION
16	表情	表情	*biǎoqíng*	n.	facial expression
17	泥塑艺术	泥塑藝術	*nísù yìshù*	n.	art of clay sculpture
18	顶峰	頂峰	*dǐngfēng*	n.	high point, pinnacle
19	增添	增添	*zēngtiān*	v.	to add, to increase
20	光彩	光彩	*guāngcǎi*	n.	splendor

Questions

1 Which of the following statements is not true?

A. Xi'an was known in ancient times as Chang'an.

B. Xi'an was the capital city of over ten dynasties.

C. Xi'an was modeled after the city of Rome.

D. Xi'an was the starting point of the Silk Road.

2 Which of the following statements about the Vault of Warriors and Horses is true?

A. It has been called an "Eighth Wonder of the World."

B. It is divided into three separate vaults.

C. It contains life-sized statues of warriors and horses.

D. All of the above.

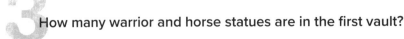

3 How many warrior and horse statues are in the first vault?

A. Exactly 14,260.
B. Over 6,000.
C. Over 1,000.
D. Exactly 230.

DISCUSSION

1. 如果要了解中国几千年的历史，为什么应该去西安？

   如果要了解中國幾千年的歷史，為什麼應該去西安？

2. 秦始皇陵的兵马俑坑为什么那么有名?

   秦始皇陵的兵馬俑坑為什麼那麼有名？

3. Using resources online, do some research about Xi'an's city wall (城墙 / 城牆). How is it similar to or different from the Great Wall of China?

4. Choose one of the following sites in and around Xi'an to research and share your findings with your class: the Great Mosque of Xi'an (清真寺), Huimin Street (回民街) the Giant Wild Goose Pagoda (大雁塔), the Small Wild Goose Pagoda (小雁塔), or the Famen Temple (法门寺 / 法門寺). What do these sites represent about Xi'an as a major stop along the Silk Road?

敦煌石窟

9

Dunhuang Rock Caves

敦煌石窟
敦煌石窟

Dūnhuáng Shíkū

敦

煌位于甘肃省的西部，是中国古代丝绸之路的必经之地。敦煌最有名的是它的石窟和艺术。敦煌共有552个石窟，以莫高窟为中心的敦煌石窟，是世界有名的古迹之一。敦煌莫高窟有上下五层，长1600米，有壁画五万多平方米。

这些壁画包括佛像画、故事画、山水画，等等。造像都是泥制彩塑，分为单身像和群像。最大的高33米，最小的只有0.1米。人们说，如果把莫高窟所有的壁画连接起来，会有25公里长。在艺术上，这些壁画不仅体现了中国的民族风格，而且吸取了印度、希腊、伊朗等国古代艺术之长。

敦煌壁画主要是一种宗教艺术，它描绘了神的形象、神的活动、神与神的关系、神与人的关系。但有的壁画也表现了人们敦煌位于甘肅省的西部，是中國古代絲綢之路的必經之地。敦煌最有名的是它的石窟和藝術。敦煌共有552個石窟，以莫高窟為中心的敦煌石窟，是世界有名的古蹟之一。敦煌莫高窟有上下五層，長1600米，有壁畫五萬多平方米。

這些壁畫包括佛像畫、故事畫、山水畫，等等。造像都是泥製彩塑，分為單身像和群像。最大的高33米，最小的只有0.1米。人們說，如果把莫高窟所有的壁畫連接起來，會有25公里長。在藝術上，這些壁畫不僅體現了中國的民族風格，而且吸取了印度、希臘、伊朗等國古代藝術之長。

敦煌壁畫主要是一種宗教藝術，它描繪了神的形象、神的活動、神與神的關系、神與人的關系。但有的壁畫也表現了人們

打猎、织布、建造房屋等活动。历史上有名的丝绸之路也出现在这些壁画中。

敦煌飞天也是敦煌艺术之一，它主要是靠飘曳的衣裙、飞舞的彩带而凌空翱翔的飞天。敦煌飞天非常美丽，是敦煌艺术的主要标志。

打獵、織布、建造房屋等活動。歷史上有名的絲綢之路也出現在這些壁畫中。

敦煌飛天也是敦煌藝術之一，它主要是靠飄曳的衣裙、飛舞的彩帶而凌空翱翔的飛天。敦煌飛天非常美麗，是敦煌藝術的主要標誌。

Vocabulary List

	SIMPLIFIED CHARACTERS	TRADITIONAL CHARACTERS	PINYIN	PART OF SPEECH	ENGLISH DEFINITION
1	敦煌	敦煌	*Dūnhuáng*	pn.	(name of a place)
2	石窟	石窟	*shíkū*	n.	stone cave
3	莫高窟	莫高窟	*Mògāo Kū*	pn.	Mogao Caves
4	壁画	壁畫	*bìhuà*	n.	mural paintings
5	造像	造像	*zàoxiàng*	n.	statue
6	泥制彩塑	泥製彩塑	*nízhì cǎisù*	n.	colored clay sculpture
7	单身像	單身像	*dānshēn xiàng*	n.	statue of a single figure
8	群像	群像	*qúnxiàng*	n.	statues of a group
9	米	米	*mǐ*	n.	meter
10	民族风格	民族風格	*mínzú fēnggé*	n.	folk style
11	吸取	吸取	*xīqǔ*	v.	to absorb, to draw from, to assimilate
12	印度	印度	*Yìndù*	pn.	India
13	希腊	希臘	*Xīlà*	pn.	Greece
14	伊朗	伊朗	*Yīlǎng*	pn.	Iran
15	宗教	宗教	*zōngjiào*	n.	religion

	SIMPLIFIED CHARACTERS	TRADITIONAL CHARACTERS	PINYIN	PART OF SPEECH	ENGLISH DEFINITION
16	关系	關係	*guānxi*	n.	relation, relationship
17	打猎	打獵	*dǎliè*	v.	to hunt
18	飞天	飛天	*fēitiān*	pn.	flying *apsaras* (Buddhist deities/ devas)
19	飘曳	飄曳	*piāoyè*	adj.	floating, fluttering
20	凌空	凌空	*língkōng*	vo.	to rise high up in the air
21	翱翔	翱翔	*áoxiáng*	v.	to soar, to hover
22	标志	標誌	*biāozhì*	n.	sign, symbol

Questions

1 About how many square meters of mural paintings are in the Mogao Caves?

A. 5
B. 552
C. 1,600
D. 50,000

2 The Dunhuang mural paintings exhibit artistic influences from

A. India, Greece, and Iran.
B. India, Greece, and Mongolia.
C. Nepal, India, and Greece.
D. Nepal, India, and Mongolia.

Which of the following are not depicted in the Dunhuang mural paintings?

A. Relationships between gods.

B. Gods hunting, weaving cloth, and building houses.

C. Relationships between gods and humans.

D. People hunting, weaving cloth, and building houses.

DISCUSSION

1. 敦煌在中国的什么地方？它为什么很
有名？

   敦煌在中國的什麼地方？它為什麼很
有名？

2. 除了描写宗教以外，敦煌壁画还描写
什么？

   除了描寫宗教以外，敦煌壁畫還描寫
什麼？

3. What is the origin of the Dunhuang mural paintings?

4. How do the Dunhuang mural paintings reflect the historical and geographical significance of the city? Can you think of other places in the world of similar significance that are represented by their artwork or architecture?

西藏布达拉宫
西藏布達拉宮

10

Tibet's Potala Palace

西藏布达拉宫
西藏布達拉宮

Xīzàng Bùdálā Gōng

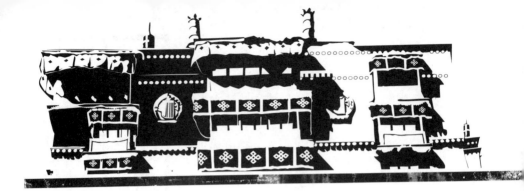

布达拉宫位于西藏拉萨市西北郊区，海拔3700多米，主楼高117米，共13层，是世界上海拔最高、规模最大的宫殿式建筑群。布达拉宫始建于公元7世纪，已有1300年的历史。在信仰藏传佛教的人民心中，这座小山就像观音菩萨居住的普陀山，因而人们用藏语称此为布达拉，就是普陀之意。布达拉宫是世界十大土木建筑之一，也是中华民族古建筑的精华之作。布达拉宫集中表现了西藏的宗教、政治、历史和艺术，可以说是西藏的历史博物馆。

布达拉宫的雕塑艺术融合了汉、印度和尼泊尔等佛教艺术技法，宫内集中了大量珍品。金、银、铜、铁等金属塑像数量最多，也有泥塑重彩、木雕、石刻。作品造型精美，大的有十多米高，小的只有几厘米高。

今天的布达拉宫，不论是从它的建筑方式，还是从它的文化内涵来看，都是非常独特的。人们认为，布达拉宫是汉藏艺术交流融合的结晶，是宗教艺术的宝库。

布達拉宮位於西藏拉薩市西北郊區，海拔3700多米，主樓高117米，共13層，是世界上海拔最高、規模最大的宮殿式建築群。布達拉宮始建於公元7世紀，已有1300年的歷史。在信仰藏傳佛教的人民心中，這座小山就像觀音菩薩居住的普陀山，因而人們用藏語稱此為布達拉，就是普陀之意。布達拉宮是世界十大土木建築之一，也是中華民族古建築的精華之作。布達拉宮集中表現了西藏的宗教、政治、歷史和藝術，可以說是西藏的歷史博物館。

布達拉宮的雕塑藝術融合了漢、印度和尼泊爾等佛教藝術技法，宮內集中了大量珍品。金、銀、銅、鐵等金屬塑像數量最多，也有泥塑重彩、木雕、石刻。作品造型精美，大的有十多米高，小的只有幾厘米高。

今天的布達拉宮，不論是從它的建築方式，還是從它的文化內涵來看，都是非常獨特的。人們認為，布達拉宮是漢藏藝術交流融合的結晶，是宗教藝術的寶庫。

Vocabulary List

	SIMPLIFIED CHARACTERS	TRADITIONAL CHARACTERS	PINYIN	PART OF SPEECH	ENGLISH DEFINITION
1	布达拉宫	布達拉宫	Bùdálā Gōng	pn.	Potala Palace
2	西藏	西藏	Xīzàng	pn.	Tibet
3	拉萨市	拉薩市	Lāsà Shì	pn.	Lhasa city
4	海拔	海拔	hǎibá	n.	height above sea level
5	主楼	主樓	zhǔ lóu	n.	main building
6	规模	規模	guīmó	n.	scale, dimension
7	宫殿式	宫殿式	gōngdiàn shì	adj.	palace-style
8	建筑群	建築群	jiànzhù qún	n.	group of buildings
9	公元	公元	gōngyuán	n.	the Common Era
10	世纪	世紀	shìjì	n.	century
11	信仰	信仰	xìnyǎng	n.	faith, belief
12	藏传佛教	藏傳佛教	Zàngchuán Fójiào	pn.	Tibetan Buddhism

	SIMPLIFIED CHARACTERS	TRADITIONAL CHARACTERS	PINYIN	PART OF SPEECH	ENGLISH DEFINITION
13	观音菩萨	觀音菩薩	*Guānyīn Púsà*	pn.	Bodhisattva Guanyin
14	居住	居住	*jūzhù*	v.	to reside
15	普陀山	普陀山	*Pǔtuó Shān*	pn.	Mount Putuo
16	藏语	藏語	*Zàngyǔ*	pn.	Tibetan language
17	土木建筑	土木建築	*tǔmù jiànzhù*	n.	construction
18	精华	精華	*jīnghuá*	n.	essence
19	雕塑	雕塑	*diāosù*	n.	sculpture
20	融合	融合	*rónghé*	v.	to merge, to mix together
21	尼泊尔	尼泊爾	*Níbó'ěr*	pn.	Nepal
22	珍品	珍品	*zhēnpǐn*	n.	treasure
23	铜	銅	*tóng*	n.	copper
24	铁	鐵	*tiě*	n.	iron
25	金属	金屬	*jīnshǔ*	n.	metal

	SIMPLIFIED CHARACTERS	TRADITIONAL CHARACTERS	PINYIN	PART OF SPEECH	ENGLISH DEFINITION
26	木雕	木雕	*mùdiāo*	n.	wooden sculpture
27	石刻	石刻	*shíkè*	n.	stone inscription
28	造型	造型	*zàoxíng*	n.	shape, mold
29	精美	精美	*jīngměi*	adj.	elegant
30	厘米	厘米	*límǐ*	n.	centimeter
31	内涵	內涵	*nèihán*	n.	connotation, intention
32	独特	獨特	*dútè*	adj.	unique
33	交流	交流	*jiāoliú*	v.	to exchange
34	结晶	結晶	*jiéjīng*	n.	result, crystallization
35	宝库	寶庫	*bǎokù*	n.	treasure trove

Questions

1 Which of the following statements about the Potala Palace is false?

A. It is built at an altitude of over 3,700 meters.

B. The main building is 117 meters tall.

C. It is built at an altitude of 117 meters.

D. The main building contains 13 floors.

2 How did the Potala Palace get its name?

A. It is located on Mount Potala.

B. It resembles the Bodhisattva Guanyin.

C. It is located near Mount Potala.

D. It resembles the mountain where the Bodhisattva Guanyin lived.

3 Most of the sculptures at the Potala Palace are

A. in a Chinese style.

B. gold, silver, bronze, or steel.

C. the same height.

D. clay, wood, or stone.

1. 为什么说布达拉宫是"西藏的历史
   博物馆"？
   為什麼說布達拉宮是"西藏的歷史
   博物館"？

2. 布达拉宫有什么艺术珍品？
   布達拉宮有什麼藝術珍品？

3. What do the styles of architecture and art at Potala Palace
   indicate about the history and spread of Buddhism?

4. How does Buddhism as it is practiced in Tibet and other
   parts of China compare to and contrast with Confucianism
   and Daoism?

III

Love Stories

第三章 愛情故事

This unit contains four famous romantic tales, each representing a different type of Chinese love story. For example, "Giving One's Best in a Time of Hardship" (相濡以沫) shows how animals in nature can make sacrifices for one another out of love. Other stories depict the affection between humans and animals, such as "The Deer Looks Back" (鹿回头 / 鹿回頭), symbolizing the relationship between humans and nature. Some stories, such as "A Broken Mirror Repairs Itself" (破镜重圆 / 破镜重圓), come from historical events or legends, many of which reflect how love can endure tremendous hardships. Lastly, tragedies such as "The Conqueror Bids Farewell to His Favorite Concubine" (霸王别姬 / 霸王別姬) have been adapted into operas, plays, and films.

11

Giving One's Best in a Time of Hardship

相濡以沫
相濡以沫

Xiāng rú yǐ mò

从前，有两条鱼在一条河里生活着，它们相亲相爱，过着快乐的日子。可是有一年夏天，雨下得很少，河流在慢慢地干枯。这两条鱼非常忧虑，它们必须赶快找到新的河流，要不然，很快就要干死了。

它们先往河的下游游去。但是，越往下游，水却越少了，最后它们游到了一片泥土上。前面没有路了，它们只能往回游。可是它们刚转过身，却发现河流已经不存在了。只有较低的地方有浅浅的水洼。

第一天，它们可以在水洼里翻身。

第二天，它们只能侧身挤在一起。

第三天，猛烈的太阳把水全吸干了。它们全身火辣辣的。丈夫望着虚弱的妻子，心里很难过。它用尽最后的力气，将自己口中的一点点唾沫吐在它身上，希望能滋润

從前

，有兩條魚在一條河裡生活著，它們相親相愛，過著快樂的日子。可是有一年夏天，雨下得很少，河流在慢慢地乾枯。這兩條魚非常憂慮，它們必須趕快找到新的河流，要不然，很快就要乾死了。

它們先往河的下游游去。但是，越往下游，水卻越少了，最後它們游到了一片泥土上。前面沒有路了，它們只能往回游。可是它們剛轉過身，卻發現河流已經不存在了。只有較低的地方有淺淺的水窪。

第一天，它們可以在水窪裡翻身。

第二天，它們只能側身擠在一起。

第三天，猛烈的太陽把水全吸乾了。它們全身火辣辣的。丈夫望著虛弱的妻子，

它一段时间。妻子还以为下雨了，高兴极了。但是它看见太阳仍然很强烈，而且丈夫的身上有很多血丝。妻子奋力靠近丈夫，将自己的唇贴到它身上，吃力地挤出最后的一点唾沫。丈夫已经没有力气了。唯一能做到的，就是张开嘴，衔住妻子的尾鳍。妻子也同样衔住丈夫的尾鳍。

就这样，它们一天天变小，干枯，最后成了一对枯鱼，一对相爱到死，永不分离的爱人。人们被这个故事深深感动了，因为他们相信这对夫妻是一对真正地相爱到永远的爱人。后来，人们常常用相濡以沫这个成语，来比喻同处于困境而互相尽微力救助的夫妻。

心裡很難過。它用盡最後的力氣，將自己口中的一點點唾沫吐在它身上，希望能滋潤它一段時間。妻子還以為下雨了，高興極了。但是它看見太陽仍然很強烈，而且丈夫的身上有很多血絲。妻子奮力靠近丈夫，將自己的唇貼到它身上，吃力地擠出最後的一點唾沫。

丈夫已經沒有力氣了。唯一能做到的，就是張開嘴，銜住妻子的尾鰭。妻子也同樣銜住丈夫的尾鰭。

就這樣，它們一天天變小，乾枯，最後成了一對枯魚，一對相愛到死，永不分離的愛人。人們被這個故事深深感動了，因為他們相信這對夫妻是一對真正地相愛到永遠的愛人。後來，人們常常用相濡以沫這個成語，來比喻同處於困境而互相盡微力救助的夫妻。

Vocabulary List

	SIMPLIFIED CHARACTERS	TRADITIONAL CHARACTERS	PINYIN	PART OF SPEECH	ENGLISH DEFINITION
1	干枯	乾枯	*gānkū*	adj./v.	dried up; to dry up
2	忧虑	憂慮	*yōulǜ*	v.	to worry
3	下游	下游	*xiàyóu*	n.	lower reaches of a river
4	泥土	泥土	*nítǔ*	n.	soil
5	存在	存在	*cúnzài*	v.	to exist
6	较低	較低	*jiàodī*	adj.	lower
7	浅浅的	淺淺的	*qiǎnqiǎnde*	adj.	shallow
8	水洼	水窪	*shuǐwā*	n.	puddle, pool
9	翻身	翻身	*fān shēn*	vo.	to turn over
10	侧身	側身	*cè shēn*	vo.	to lie on one's side
11	吸干	吸乾	*xīgān*	vc.	to absorb, to suck up completely

	SIMPLIFIED CHARACTERS	TRADITIONAL CHARACTERS	PINYIN	PART OF SPEECH	ENGLISH DEFINITION
12	火辣辣	火辣辣	*huǒlàlà*	adj.	burning hot
13	虚弱	虛弱	*xūruò*	adj.	weak, feeble
14	难过	難過	*nánguò*	adj.	sad, sorrowful
15	用尽	用盡	*yòngjìn*	vc.	to use up completely
16	唾沫	唾沫	*tuòmo*	n.	saliva, spittle
17	吐	吐	*tǔ*	v.	to spit
18	滋润	滋潤	*zīrùn*	v.	to moisten
19	血丝	血絲	*xuèsī*	n.	blood stain
20	奋力	奮力	*fèn lì*	vo.	to do all one can
21	靠近	靠近	*kàojìn*	vc.	to draw close
22	唇	唇	*chún*	n.	lips

	SIMPLIFIED CHARACTERS	TRADITIONAL CHARACTERS	PINYIN	PART OF SPEECH	ENGLISH DEFINITION
23	唯一	唯一	*wéiyī*	adj.	only
24	衔住	銜住	*xiánzhù*	vc.	to hold in the mouth
25	尾鳍	尾鰭	*wěiqí*	n.	tail fin
26	永不分离	永不分離	*yǒngbù fēnlí*	expr.	to never separate, to be together forever
27	成语	成語	*chéngyǔ*	n.	idiom, phrase
28	比喻	比喻	*bǐyù*	n./v.	metaphor; to metaphorize
29	处于困境	處於困境	*chǔyú kùnjìng*	expr.	to be in a predicament
30	尽微力救助	盡微力救助	*jìn wēilì jiùzhù*	expr.	to help with all one's might

The two fish in the river had to find another place to live because

A. there was little rain and the river was drying up.

B. the hot weather made the water too warm.

C. there was too much rain and the river was overflowing.

D. the cold weather made the water too cold.

To keep his wife alive for a little longer, the husband fish

A. used his last bit of strength to push her into another river.

B. shielded her from the hot sun.

C. used his last bit of strength to keep her wet with his saliva.

D. covered her in the mud.

The fish's wife was happy because she

A. was moved by her husband's actions.

B. thought it was raining.

C. saw that the sun was setting.

D. found another river nearby.

When the fish's wife saw what was happening to her husband, she

A. drew close to him to cover his wounds.

B. put her lips on his wounds to heal them.

C. drew close to him to give him shade from the sun.

D. put her lips on his body to keep it moist.

相濡以沫 giving one's best in a time of hardship

5 The idiom that comes from this story is used to describe

A. the importance of being prepared.

B. helping others with all one's might in a predicament.

C. the importance of conserving resources.

D. helping yourself before others in a predicament.

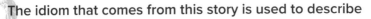

DISCUSSION

1. 这对夫妻遇到了什么困难？

這對夫妻遇到了什麼困難？

2. 在困难中他们怎样互相帮助？

在困難中他們怎樣互相幫助？

3. This story originally comes from the writings of Zhuangzi, a famous Daoist philosopher. Using resources online, identify the key elements of his philosophy. How is he similar to or different from Confucius?

4. This story is one of many instances in Chinese literature of using an example from nature to impart wisdom. Can you think of a story from another culture that similarly uses animals to teach a lesson?

12

The Deer Looks Back

鹿回头
鹿回頭

Lù huí tóu

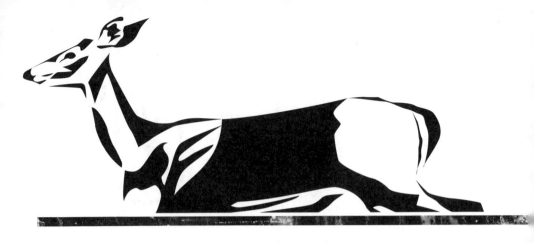

很久以前，有一个风景美丽的山村，里面住着很多农民和猎手。阿黑是一个年轻的猎手，家里很穷，他跟母亲生活在一起。有一天，阿黑出去打猎，发现了一只美丽的花鹿，可是这只花鹿正被一只豹子紧追不舍。阿黑爬到树上，等待时机，把豹子射死了。花鹿继续向前飞跑，阿黑紧紧地追赶着。就这样，他们一直跑了九天九夜，翻过了九十九座山，走过了九十九条河。最后，他们到了海边的悬崖上，花鹿面对大海，无路可逃，只能望着前方。

这时，阿黑的心里很矛盾。他想搭弓射箭，可是被这美丽的景色打动了，手里的箭射不出去。就在这时候，花鹿突然回头，充满深情地望着阿黑，阿黑更加迟疑了。就在阿黑迟疑的时候，突然电光一闪，接着出现一团白色的烟雾。然后，花鹿不见了，

很久以前，有一個風景美麗的山村，裡面住著很多農民和獵手。阿黑是一個年輕的獵手，家裡很窮，他跟母親生活在一起。有一天，阿黑出去打獵，發現了一隻美麗的花鹿，可是這隻花鹿正被一隻豹子緊追不捨。阿黑爬到樹上，等待時機，把豹子射死了。花鹿繼續向前飛跑，阿黑緊緊地追趕著。就這樣，他們一直跑了九天九夜，翻過了九十九座山，走過了九十九條河。最後，他們到了海邊的懸崖上，花鹿面對大海，無路可逃，只能望著前方。

這時，阿黑的心裡很矛盾。他想搭弓射箭，可是被這美麗的景色打動了，手裡的箭射不出去。就在這時候，花鹿突然回頭，充滿深情地望著阿黑，阿黑更加遲疑了。就在阿黑遲疑的時候，突然電光一閃，接著

只见一位美丽的姑娘向阿黑慢慢地走过来。阿黑放下手中的箭，一瞬间爱上了这位美丽的花鹿姑娘，花鹿姑娘也爱上了阿黑。

阿黑和花鹿姑娘很快结婚了。从此，他们过着幸福的生活。后来，为了纪念他们美丽的爱情，人们把那个悬崖叫作"鹿回头"。

出現一團白色的煙霧。然後，
花鹿不見了，只見一位美麗的
姑娘向阿黑慢慢地走過來。
阿黑放下手中的箭，一瞬間愛
上了這位美麗的花鹿姑娘，
花鹿姑娘也愛上了阿黑。

　　阿黑和花鹿姑娘很快結
婚了。從此，他們過著幸福的
生活。後來，為了紀念他們美
麗的愛情，人們把那個懸崖叫
作"鹿回頭"。

Vocabulary List

	SIMPLIFIED CHARACTERS	TRADITIONAL CHARACTERS	PINYIN	PART OF SPEECH	ENGLISH DEFINITION
1	猎手	獵手	*lièshǒu*	n.	hunter
2	花鹿	花鹿	*huālù*	n.	spotted deer
3	豹子	豹子	*bàozi*	n.	leopard
4	紧追不舍	緊追不捨	*jǐnzhuī bùshě*	expr.	to chase closely
5	等待时机	等待時機	*děngdài shíjī*	vo.	to wait for an opportunity
6	继续	繼續	*jìxù*	v.	to continue
7	翻过	翻過	*fānguò*	vc.	to climb over
8	悬崖	懸崖	*xuányá*	n.	overhanging cliff
9	无路可逃	無路可逃	*wúlù kětáo*	expr.	no way out
10	矛盾	矛盾	*máodùn*	adj.	indecisive, contradictory
11	搭弓	搭弓	*dā gōng*	vo.	to put the arrow on the bow
12	射箭	射箭	*shè jiàn*	vo.	to shoot an arrow
13	充满深情	充滿深情	*chōngmǎn shēnqíng*	vo.	to be full of deep love and emotion
14	迟疑	遲疑	*chíyí*	v.	to hesitate

	SIMPLIFIED CHARACTERS	TRADITIONAL CHARACTERS	PINYIN	PART OF SPEECH	ENGLISH DEFINITION
15	电光一闪	電光一閃	diànguāng yīshǎn	expr.	a sudden flash of lightning
16	烟雾	煙霧	yānwù	n.	smoke and fog
17	一瞬间	一瞬間	yīshùnjiān	adv.	all of a sudden

Questions

1 **Which of the following is not true about Ah Hei?**

A. His family was very poor.

B. He lived with his father.

C. He was a young hunter.

D. He lived in a mountain village.

2 **When Ah Hei first discovered the deer, it was**

A. chasing a leopard.

B. fighting a leopard.

C. being chased by a leopard.

D. hiding from a leopard.

3 **When Ah Hei killed the leopard, the deer**

A. stopped running.

B. looked back at him.

C. flew into the air.

D. continued running.

4 Why couldn't Ah Hei go through with killing the deer when it stopped at the cliff?

A. He was moved by the beautiful scene.
B. He did not want the deer to fall.
C. He felt bad for the deer.
D. He had already killed the leopard.

5 What happened when the deer looked back at Ah Hei?

A. He turned into a deer and continued chasing her in the mountains.
B. She turned into a beautiful girl and they fell in love.
C. He slowly approached the deer and brought it back to safety.
D. She suddenly disappeared in a cloud of white smoke.

DISCUSSION

1. 你认为阿黑在花鹿的眼睛里看到了什么?
   你認為阿黑在花鹿的眼睛裡看到了什麼？

2. 你认为这个故事的寓意是什么?
   你認為這個故事的寓意是什麼？

3. What do you think the significance is of Ah Hei chasing after the deer for nine days and nine nights, climbing over ninety-nine mountains and crossing ninety-nine rivers? Do these numbers carry a special meaning? Consider the different homophones associated with the number nine in Chinese.

4. In China, there is a mountain and a park named after this story. Using resources online, find out where the site is located in China. What does the statue in the park depict? How might the story and its landmark relate to protecting nature?

13

A Broken Mirror Repairs Itself

破镜重圆
破鏡重圓

Pò jìng chóng yuán

古时候，中国有一个小国家叫陈国。陈国的国王有一个妹妹，叫乐昌公主，她和她的丈夫徐德言相亲相爱，过着幸福的生活。但是陈国的国王很腐败，徐德言非常忧虑。有一天，丈夫对妻子说："战争随时会来，到时候我们很有可能不能在一起。但只要我们活着，总会有见面的机会。我们应该留下一件东西，作为将来见面的凭证。"

徐德言拿来一面镜子，把它分作两半，一半自己留下，一半交给妻子。他告诉妻子一定要好好保存，并对她说："如果我们分开了，每年正月十五日那天，你让人把这半面镜子拿到市场上去卖。只要我还活着，我一定想办法到市场上去打听。我会以我的半面镜子为凭证，来和你团聚。"

不久，陈国果然被敌人攻陷了。乐昌公主被抓走了，徐德言也被迫逃走了。后来古時候，中國有一個小國家叫陳國。陳國的國王有一個妹妹，叫<u>樂昌公主</u>，她和她的丈夫<u>徐德言</u>相親相愛，過著幸福的生活。但是陳國的國王很腐敗，<u>徐德言</u>非常憂慮。有一天，丈夫對妻子說："戰爭隨時會來，到時候我們很有可能不能在一起。但只要我們活著，總會有見面的機會。我們應該留下一件東西，作為將來見面的憑證。"

<u>徐德言</u>拿來一面鏡子，把它分作兩半，一半自己留下，一半交給妻子。他告訴妻子一定要好好保存，並對她說："如果我們分開了，每年正月十五日那天，你讓人把這半面鏡子拿到市場上去賣。只要我還活著，我一定想辦法到市場上去打聽。我會以我的半面鏡子為憑證，來和你團聚。"

徐德言听说妻子去了一个很远的城市，便不顾艰难地赶到那里，寻找妻子。他总是拿出他的半面镜子，想念着妻子。而乐昌公主也经常抚摸着她的那半面镜子，想念着丈夫。

正月十五日终于到了。徐德言赶到市场，看见一个仆人来回走动，高价叫卖半面镜子。徐德言拿起镜子仔细看了看，认出这就是妻子手中的那一半。于是徐德言在镜子上写了一首诗，交给这个仆人带回。乐昌公主见到丈夫写的诗以后，整天哭泣，不吃不喝。抓走她的人知道这件事以后，非常感动。他们找到徐德言，让他把乐昌公主带走，还给了他们很多东西。这一对夫妻终于得以团聚。后来，人们常用"破镜重圆"来比喻分离以后又重聚的夫妻。

不久，陳國果然被敵人攻陷了。樂昌公主被抓走了，徐德言也被迫逃走了。後來徐德言聽說妻子去了一個很遠的城市，便不顧艱難地趕到那裡，尋找妻子。他總是拿出他的半面鏡子，想念著妻子。而樂昌公主也經常撫摸著她的那半面鏡子，想念著丈夫。

正月十五日終於到了。徐德言趕到市場，看見一個僕人來回走動，高價叫賣半面鏡子。徐德言拿起鏡子仔細看了看，認出這就是妻子手中的那一半。於是徐德言在鏡子上寫了一首詩，交給這個僕人帶回。樂昌公主見到丈夫寫的詩以後，整天哭泣，不吃不喝。抓走她的人知道這件事以後，非常感動。他們找到徐德言，讓他把樂昌公主帶走，還給了他們很多東西。這一對夫妻終於得以團聚。後來，人們常用"破鏡重圓"來比喻分離以後又重聚的夫妻。

Vocabulary List

	SIMPLIFIED CHARACTERS	TRADITIONAL CHARACTERS	PINYIN	PART OF SPEECH	ENGLISH DEFINITION
1	公主	公主	*gōngzhǔ*	n.	princess
2	腐败	腐敗	*fǔbài*	adj.	corrupt
3	随时	隨時	*suíshí*	adv.	at any time
4	面	面	*miàn*	mw.	(measure word for mirrors)
5	镜子	鏡子	*jìngzi*	n.	mirror
6	凭证	憑證	*píngzhèng*	n.	proof, evidence
7	攻陷	攻陷	*gōngxiàn*	v.	to storm, to capture
8	抓走	抓走	*zhuāzǒu*	vc.	to arrest, to catch
9	被迫	被迫	*bèipò*	v.	to be forced
10	逃走	逃走	*táozǒu*	vc.	to escape
11	不顾艰难	不顧艱難	*búgù jiānnán*	expr.	in spite of hardships
12	寻找	尋找	*xúnzhǎo*	v.	to look for
13	抚摸	撫摸	*fǔmō*	v.	to touch, to stroke
14	仆人	僕人	*púrén*	n.	servant
15	高价	高價	*gāojià*	n.	high price
16	仔细	仔細	*zǐxì*	adv.	closely, carefully
17	哭泣	哭泣	*kūqì*	v.	to cry
18	分离	分離	*fēnlí*	v.	to separate

1 Why was Xu Deyan worried about the fate of the state of Chen?

A. The king was weak.

B. His wife had angered the king.

C. The king was corrupt.

D. His wife had too little power as princess.

2 In case they were separated, Xu Deyan gave his wife

A. a mirror to sell if she needed money.

B. half of a mirror and kept the other half.

C. a broken mirror for good luck.

D. both halves of a mirror to symbolize their reunion.

3 What did Xu Deyan do when he found one of the mirror's halves?

A. He cried in grief because he knew his wife did not survive.

B. He bought it from the old man selling it at a very high price.

C. He cried with joy because he knew his wife had survived.

D. He wrote a poem on the mirror to his wife for the old man to deliver.

1. 以前的陈国在什么地方？它跟楚国有
   什么关系？

   以前的陳國在什麼地方？它跟楚國有
   什麼關係？

2. 徐德言为什么让妻子每年正月十五让人把那
   半面镜子拿到市场上去卖？这一天是什么特
   别的日子？

   徐德言為什麼讓妻子每年正月十五讓人
   把那半面鏡子拿到市場上去賣？這一天
   是什麼特別的日子？

3. How is the idiom from this story used today, and what does
   it literally mean? What is the significance of the shape of
   the mirror, and what does this shape represent in Chinese
   traditions that you have studied?

4. What do you think Xu Deyan wrote in his poem to his wife?
   Try writing your own poem with a similar message.

14

The Conqueror Bids Farewell to His Favorite Concubine

霸王別姬
霸王別姬

Xiang Yu (232–202 B.C.E.), a famous Chinese general, was born in the state of Chu, which became a territory of the Qin dynasty during its unification of China. He became the leader of the rebel forces that ultimately captured the Qin capital and overthrew its rule. In an attempt to restore the feudal kingdoms, he divided Chu among different generals, and reserved the old territory of Chu for himself along with the title of "The Conqueror" (霸王).

中国的第一个皇帝秦始皇死了以后，楚国的国王项羽跟他的对手们开始争夺权利。他带兵打仗，常常获胜，而且常常以少胜多。有一次，他带领两万多战士打败了三十多万敌人，所以人们也叫他"霸王"。

项羽有一个非常喜爱的妾，叫虞姬。虞姬长得很美丽，还会跳舞和舞剑。她也很爱项羽，常常跟他一起去打仗。大家都说，她最懂霸王的想法，也最懂霸王的心。

有一天，好几个国家联合起来，一起攻打项羽的军队，他们把项羽的军队四面包围起来，并用楚国的语言唱歌。项羽的军队以为他们的家乡已经被敌人占领了，因此人心涣散。而且他们已经没有了粮食和武器，士兵人数也大大减少。就在这个四面楚歌的晚上，项羽心里非常痛苦，他知道大势已去，自己的军队无论如何

中國的第一個皇帝<u>秦始皇</u>死了以後，楚國的國王<u>項羽</u>跟他的對手們開始爭奪權利。他帶兵打仗，常常獲勝，而且常常以少勝多。有一次，他帶領兩萬多戰士打敗了三十多萬敵人，所以人們也叫他"霸王"。

<u>項羽</u>有一個非常喜愛的妾，叫<u>虞姬</u>。<u>虞姬</u>長得很美麗，還會跳舞和舞劍。她也很愛<u>項羽</u>，常常跟他一起去打仗。大家都說，她最懂霸王的想法，也最懂霸王的心。

有一天，好幾個國家聯合起來，一起攻打<u>項羽</u>的軍隊，他們把<u>項羽</u>的軍隊四面包圍起來，並用楚國的語言唱歌。<u>項羽</u>的軍隊以為他們的家鄉已經被敵人佔領了，因此人心渙散。而且他們已經沒有了糧食和武器，士兵人數也大大減少。就在這個

都会被敌人打败。突围是死，不突围也是死。但是他还是决定突围。在突围前夕，他对着<u>虞姬</u>唱着悲壮的歌，心里很清楚自己就要跟自己心爱的<u>虞姬</u>诀别了。

据说<u>虞姬</u>为了让<u>霸王</u>能一心一意地突破敌人的包围，不为她分心，她最后一次为自己的爱人跳了一次剑舞。歌舞停了之后，<u>虞姬</u>拔剑自杀了。

<u>虞姬</u>死了以后，<u>项羽</u>开始突围。突围中，他的士兵全部战死，他一个人一边撤退，一边继续战斗。当他撤退到乌江边上时，只剩了他自己一个人。这时，他觉得对不起自己的士兵和他们的家人，他不愿意过江，也拔剑自杀了。

<u>虞姬</u>和<u>霸王</u>一起经历了战争，分享过快乐，共同面对困境，他们的爱情故事感动了很多人。

四面楚歌的晚上，項羽心裡非常痛苦，他知道大勢已去，自己的軍隊無論如何都會被敵人打敗。突圍是死，不突圍也是死。但是他還是決定突圍。在突圍前夕，他對著虞姬唱著悲壯的歌，心裡很清楚自己就要跟自己心愛的虞姬訣別了。

據說虞姬為了讓霸王能一心一意地突破敵人的包圍，不為她分心，她最後一次為自己的愛人跳了一次劍舞。歌舞停了之後，虞姬拔劍自殺了。

虞姬死了以後，項羽開始突圍。突圍中，他的士兵全部戰死，他一個人一邊撤退，一邊繼續戰鬥。當他撤退到烏江邊上時，只剩了他自己一個人。這時，他覺得對不起自己的士兵和他們的家人，他不願意過江，也拔劍自殺了。

虞姬和霸王一起經歷了戰爭，分享過快樂，共同面對困境，他們的愛情故事感動了很多人。

Vocabulary List

	SIMPLIFIED CHARACTERS	TRADITIONAL CHARACTERS	PINYIN	PART OF SPEECH	ENGLISH DEFINITION
1	项羽	項羽	*Xiàng Yǔ*	pn.	(name of a person)
2	对手	對手	*duìshǒu*	n.	opponent, adversary
3	争夺权利	爭奪權利	*zhēngduó quánlì*	vo.	to fight for power
4	带兵	帶兵	*dài bīng*	vo.	to lead the army
5	获胜	獲勝	*huò shèng*	vo.	to gain victory, to win
6	以少胜多	以少勝多	*yǐshǎo shèngduō*	expr.	to defeat many with a few
7	霸王	霸王	*Bàwáng*	pn.	The Conqueror
8	妾	妾	*qiè*	n.	concubine
9	虞姬	虞姬	*Yú Jī*	pn.	Concubine Yu
10	舞剑	舞劍	*wǔ jiàn*	vo.	to perform a sword dance
11	联合	聯合	*liánhé*	v.	to unite

	SIMPLIFIED CHARACTERS	TRADITIONAL CHARACTERS	PINYIN	PART OF SPEECH	ENGLISH DEFINITION
12	占领	佔領	*zhànlǐng*	v.	to occupy
13	人心涣散	人心渙散	*rénxīn huànsàn*	expr.	to lose popular morale
14	粮食	糧食	*liángshi*	n.	grain, food
15	武器	武器	*wǔqì*	n.	weapon, arms
16	士兵	士兵	*shìbīng*	n.	soldier
17	减少	減少	*jiǎnshǎo*	v.	to reduce
18	四面楚歌	四面楚歌	*sìmiàn chǔgē*	expr.	to be besieged on all sides
19	大势已去	大勢已去	*dàshì yǐqù*	expr.	the situation is hopeless
20	无论如何	無論如何	*wúlùn rúhé*	conj.	no matter what
21	前夕	前夕	*qiánxī*	n.	eve
22	悲壮	悲壯	*bēizhuàng*	adj.	moving and tragic

	SIMPLIFIED CHARACTERS	TRADITIONAL CHARACTERS	PINYIN	PART OF SPEECH	ENGLISH DEFINITION
23	诀别	訣別	*jué bié*	vo.	to bid farewell
24	据说	據說	*jùshuō*	conj.	it is said
25	一心一意	一心一意	*yìxīn yíyì*	expr.	heart and soul, wholeheartedly
26	分心	分心	*fēn xīn*	vo.	to divert one's attention
27	拔剑	拔劍	*bá jiàn*	vo.	to pull out a sword
28	撤退	撤退	*chètuì*	v.	to retreat
29	乌江	烏江	*Wū Jiāng*	pn.	the Wu River
30	过江	過江	*guò jiāng*	vo.	to cross the river
31	经历	經歷	*jīnglì*	v.	to experience
32	分享	分享	*fēnxiǎng*	v.	to share
33	困境	困境	*kùnjìng*	n.	predicament

Questions

1 How did Xiang Yu become known as The Conqueror?

A. He was able to defeat many adversaries even when outnumbered.

B. His enemies surrendered as soon as they saw him on the battlefield.

C. He had the largest army of all the Warring States.

D. He conquered the heart of his concubine, Lady Yu.

2 What was the main reason Xiang Yu's army lost morale?

A. They became outnumbered when the armies of several states united.

B. They were surrounded and heard victory songs from the enemy.

C. They ran out of food and weaponry, and the number of soldiers was greatly reduced.

D. They were surrounded and heard the songs of their homeland.

3 When Xiang Yu retreated to the Wu River and was the only one left to fight, he

A. jumped in the river and swam across.

B. drew his sword to meet the same fate as Lady Yu.

C. jumped in the river and drowned.

D. surrendered himself to save Lady Yu.

1. "四面楚歌"这个成语是什么意思？请用
   "四面楚歌"造句。
   "四面楚歌"這個成語是什麼意思？請用
   "四面楚歌"造句。

2. 虞姬为什么要自杀？
   虞姬為什麼要自殺？

3. Why do you think this story has become a timeless tragedy that has been adapted into films, novels, and plays? Do you notice any similarities with other famous love stories from other parts of the world?

IV

Knight-Errant Stories

第四章　武侠故事

第四章　武侠故事

Similar to the knight-errant stories of the West, the *wuxia* (武俠 / 武侠) tales of China follow the adventures of martial artists and warriors who fight for righteousness. These Chinese heroes often demonstrate qualities such as benevolence, loyalty, and courage, which are deeply admired by readers of this popular form of literature to this day. This unit features many strong female protagonists who are cultural figures that have been looked up to for generations. You may find parallels between the values held by these characters and the Confucian, Buddhist, and Daoist principles that are present throughout the *Tales and Traditions* series.

15

Sleeping on Firewood and Tasting Gall

卧薪尝胆
臥薪嘗膽

Wò xīn cháng dǎn

两千多年前，有两个小国家，一个叫吴国，一个叫越国。越国的国王叫勾践，吴国的国王叫夫差。这两个国家互相不友好，常常打仗。有一次，越国被吴国打败了，越国的国王勾践被吴国的国王夫差抓走了。夫差打算让勾践和他的妻子一起来吴国当奴仆，可是吴国的谋臣们都不同意，他们要马上处死勾践和他的妻子，并且把越国灭掉。但是，打了胜仗的夫差非常骄傲，不听大家的建议，还是要勾践来当奴仆。

很快，勾践和妻子一起来到吴国，他们穿上了破衣服，住进了破房子，给吴国养马驾车，忍受了很多痛苦。他们在吴国做了三年奴仆，终于赢得了吴王的信任，被释放回到了自己的国家。回国以后，勾践时刻不忘报仇。为了让自己不贪图舒适的生活，白天他跟农民一起下地干活，他的妻子也跟农妇兩千多年前，有兩個小國家，一個叫吳國，一個叫越國。越國的國王叫勾踐，吳國的國王叫夫差。這兩個國家互相不友好，常常打仗。有一次，越國被吳國打敗了，越國的國王勾踐被吳國的國王夫差抓走了。夫差打算讓勾踐和他的妻子一起來吳國當奴僕，可是吳國的謀臣們都不同意，他們要馬上處死勾踐和他的妻子，並且把越國滅掉。但是，打了勝仗的夫差非常驕傲，不聽大家的建議，還是要勾踐來當奴僕。

很快，勾踐和妻子一起來到吳國，他們穿上了破衣服，住進了破房子，給吳國養馬駕車，忍受了很多痛苦。他們在吳國做了三年奴僕，終於贏得了吳王的信任，被釋放回到了自己的國家。回國以後，勾踐時刻不忘報仇。為了讓自己不貪圖舒適的生活，白天他跟農民一起下地幹活，他的妻子也

一起纺纱织布，晚上他睡在柴草上"卧薪"。他还从房梁上垂下一根绳子，绳子的一端拴着一只很苦的猪胆，每天吃晚饭和上床睡觉前，勾贱都要先尝一口那个苦胆！二十年里，他天天这样，从来没有间断过。他还常常让他的士兵问他："你忘了那三年做奴仆的耻辱了吗？"

就这样，勾践和他的妻子深深地感动了越国人。他们团结起来，一起努力。十年后，越国变得非常强大，最后把吴国灭掉了，勾践也终于报了仇！这个故事告诉人们，只要吃苦耐劳，不断磨练自己的意志，就一定能成功。

跟農婦一起紡紗織布，晚上他睡在柴草上"臥薪"。他還從房梁上垂下一根繩子，繩子的一端拴著一隻很苦的豬膽，每天吃晚飯和上床睡覺前，勾踐都要先嘗一口那個苦膽！二十年裡，他天天這樣，從來沒有間斷過。他還常常讓他的士兵問他："你忘了那三年做奴僕的恥辱了嗎？"

就這樣，勾踐和他的妻子深深地感動了越國人。他們團結起來，一起努力。十年後，越國變得非常強大，最後把吳國滅掉了，勾踐也終於報了仇！這個故事告訴人們，只要吃苦耐勞，不斷磨練自己的意志，就一定能成功。

Vocabulary List

	SIMPLIFIED CHARACTERS	TRADITIONAL CHARACTERS	PINYIN	PART OF SPEECH	ENGLISH DEFINITION
1	吴国	吳國	*Wúguó*	pn.	state of Wu
2	越国	越國	*Yuèguó*	pn.	state of Yue
3	勾践	勾踐	*Gōu Jiàn*	pn.	(name of a person)
4	夫差	夫差	*Fū Chāi*	pn.	(name of a person)
5	奴仆	奴僕	*núpú*	n.	servant
6	谋臣	謀臣	*móuchén*	n.	advisor, counselor
7	处死	處死	*chǔsǐ*	v.	to put to death
8	灭掉	滅掉	*mièdiào*	vc.	to wipe out
9	养马	養馬	*yǎng mǎ*	vo.	to raise horses
10	忍受	忍受	*rěnshòu*	v.	to bear

	SIMPLIFIED CHARACTERS	TRADITIONAL CHARACTERS	PINYIN	PART OF SPEECH	ENGLISH DEFINITION
11	信任	信任	*xìnrèn*	n.	trust
12	释放	釋放	*shìfàng*	v.	to set free
13	时刻	時刻	*shíkè*	n./adv.	moment; constantly
14	报仇	報仇	*bàochóu*	v.	to revenge, to avenge
15	贪图	貪圖	*tāntú*	v.	to seek, to covet
16	纺纱	紡紗	*fǎng shā*	vo.	to spin yarn
17	柴草	柴草	*cháicǎo*	n.	firewood
18	房梁	房梁	*fángliáng*	n.	roof truss
19	垂下	垂下	*chuíxià*	vc.	to hang down
20	一端	一端	*yìduān*	n.	one end

	SIMPLIFIED CHARACTERS	TRADITIONAL CHARACTERS	PINYIN	PART OF SPEECH	ENGLISH DEFINITION
21	拴着	拴著	shuānzhe	v.	to tie
22	猪胆	豬膽	zhūdǎn	n.	gallbladder of a pig
23	尝	嘗	cháng	v.	to try, to taste
24	间断	間斷	jiànduàn	v.	to stop (doing something continuously)
25	耻辱	恥辱	chǐrǔ	n.	shame
26	深深地	深深地	shēnshēn de	adv.	deeply
27	吃苦耐劳	吃苦耐勞	chīkǔ nàiláo	expr.	to bear hardships and withstand hard work
28	不断	不斷	bùduàn	adv.	continuously
29	磨练	磨練	móliàn	v.	to temper oneself
30	意志	意志	yìzhì	n.	will

Questions

1

After defeating Gou Jian, Fu Chai

A. had him and his wife put to death.

B. made him is new military advisor.

C. let him and his wife escape to safety.

D. made him and his wife become servants.

2

Three years later, Fu Chai

A. promoted Gou Jian to raising his horses.

B. kept Gou Jian prisoner but released his wife.

C. developed trust in Gou Jian and released him.

D. kept Gou Jian as his military advisor.

3

What did Gou Jian do every day to remind himself to make his revenge?

A. He posted a picture of Fu Chai on his wall.

B. He worked in the fields, slept on firewood, and tasted gall.

C. He spun yarn and wove cloth with his wife.

D. He worked in the fields with his wife.

1. "吃苦"是什么意思？这个词语跟故事有
   什么关系？
   "吃苦"是什麼意思？這個詞語跟故事
   有什麼關係？

2. "卧薪尝胆"这个成语是什么意思？
   请用"卧薪尝胆"造句。
   "臥薪嘗膽"這個成語是什麼意思？
   請用"臥薪嘗膽"造句。

3. Do you think Gou Jian held a grudge against Fu Chai?
   Do you agree with Gou Jian's actions, or do you think
   he should have forgiven Fu Chai?

4. What do you do to remind yourself to continue working
   towards your goals? Would you take measures as
   extreme as those of Gou Jian? Why or why not?

16

Scraping the Poisoned Bone for Treatment

关公刮骨疗毒

關公刮骨療毒

Guān Gōng guāgǔ liáodú

中国历史上有很多很多名人，但只有两个人被称为"圣人"。一个是<u>孔子</u>，人们叫他"文圣"；另一个是<u>关公</u>，人们称他为"武圣"。<u>关公</u>是三国时期的大将军，也是人们心目中的大英雄。无论过去还是现在，人们都很崇拜他，因为他很勇敢，还有很多高尚的品质。

有一次，<u>关公</u>在战争中被敌人的毒箭射中，胳膊被刺穿了。他的士兵们要他赶快回家治疗，但他坚决不离开战场。士兵们只好到处找医生给他看病。有一个叫<u>华佗</u>的医生，知道<u>关公</u>受伤以后，赶快来为他治疗。那时候，<u>关公</u>的胳膊已经疼得难以忍受，但为了不让人发现他的痛苦，他用下棋的办法来分散自己的注意力。

<u>华佗</u>看了<u>关公</u>的箭伤后，要把<u>关公</u>的手臂牢牢地绑在柱子上，然后用刀把皮肉割开直到看见骨头，再刮去骨头上的毒，

中國歷史上有很多很多名人，但只有兩個人被稱為"聖人"。一個是孔子，人們叫他"文聖"；另一個是關公，人們稱他為"武聖"。關公是三國時期的大將軍，也是人們心目中的大英雄。無論過去還是現在，人們都很崇拜他，因為他很勇敢，還有很多高尚的品質。

　　有一次，關公在戰爭中被敵人的毒箭射中，胳膊被刺穿了。他的士兵們要他趕快回家治療，但他堅決不離開戰場。士兵們只好到處找醫生給他看病。有一個叫華佗的醫生，知道關公受傷以後，趕快來為他治療。那時候，關公的胳膊已經疼得難以忍受，但為了不讓人發現他的痛苦，他用下棋的辦法來分散自己的注意力。

　　華佗看了關公的箭傷後，要把關公的手臂牢牢地綁在柱子上，然後用刀把皮肉割開直到看見骨頭，再刮去骨頭上的毒，

敷上药，最后用线缝起来。他对关公说："这样会非常疼，就怕您忍受不了。"

关公听了，笑着说自己从来都不怕痛，更不用把胳膊绑在柱子上。然后他叫人送上饭菜，让医生先吃些东西。关公看华佗吃完了饭，就伸出了胳膊，说："现在您开始动手吧，我继续喝酒、吃饭、下棋，请先生不要介意！"

武圣关公

华佗也不再说什么，他取出一把尖刀，请人在关公的胳膊下方放上一个盆子，看准了位置，一下子把关公的皮肉割开。关公脸上的表情没有一点变化。华佗接着用刀来回刮骨头上的毒，发出悉悉的声音。伤口流出的血几乎装满了整个盆子。在场的其他将军和战士见到这个情景，没有不害怕的，只有关公自己继续下棋，又说又笑，一点都看不出他正经历着异常的痛苦。

这个故事告诉人们，关公是多么的勇敢无畏！他是一位真正的大将军和武圣。

敷上藥，最後用線縫起來。他對關公說：
"這樣會非常疼，就怕您忍受不了。"

　　關公聽了，笑著說自己從來都不怕痛，更不用把胳膊綁在柱子上。然後他叫人送上飯菜，讓醫生先吃些東西。關公看華佗吃完了飯，就伸出了胳膊，說："現在您開始動手吧，我繼續喝酒、吃飯、下棋，請先生不要介意！"

　　華佗也不再說什麼，他取出一把尖刀，請人在關公的胳膊下方放上一個盆子，看準了位置，一下子把關公的皮肉割開。關公臉上的表情沒有一點變化。華佗接著用刀來回刮骨頭上的毒，發出悉悉的聲音。傷口流出的血幾乎裝滿了整個盆子。在場的其他將軍和戰士見到這個情景，沒有不害怕的，只有關公自己繼續下棋，又說又笑，一點都看不出他正經歷著異常的痛苦。

　　這個故事告訴人們，關公是多麼的勇敢無畏！他是一位真正的大將軍和武聖。

Vocabulary List

	SIMPLIFIED CHARACTERS	TRADITIONAL CHARACTERS	PINYIN	PART OF SPEECH	ENGLISH DEFINITION
1	圣人	聖人	*shèngrén*	n.	sage
2	文圣	文聖	*Wénshèng*	pn.	Sage of Culture
3	武圣	武聖	*Wǔshèng*	pn.	Sage of War
4	三国	三國	*Sānguó*	pn.	the Three Kingdoms
5	心目	心目	*xīnmù*	n.	mind, point of view
6	崇拜	崇拜	*chóngbài*	v.	to worship
7	高尚	高尚	*gāoshàng*	adj.	noble
8	品质	品質	*pǐnzhì*	n.	quality
9	毒箭	毒箭	*dújiàn*	n.	poisoned arrow
10	治疗	治療	*zhìliáo*	v.	to treat (medically)
11	坚决	堅決	*jiānjué*	adv.	firmly
12	华佗	華佗	*Huà Tuó*	pn.	(name of a person)
13	难以忍受	難以忍受	*nányǐ rěnshòu*	expr.	hard to bear
14	下棋	下棋	*xià qí*	vo.	to play chess

	SIMPLIFIED CHARACTERS	TRADITIONAL CHARACTERS	PINYIN	PART OF SPEECH	ENGLISH DEFINITION
15	分散	分散	fēnsàn	v.	to distract
16	注意力	注意力	zhùyìlì	n.	attention
17	牢牢地	牢牢地	láoláo de	adv.	tightly
18	绑	綁	bǎng	v.	to bind, to tie
19	柱子	柱子	zhùzi	n.	pillar
20	皮肉	皮肉	píròu	n.	flesh
21	割开	隔開	gēkāi	vc.	to cut open
22	骨头	骨頭	gǔtou	n.	bone
23	刮去	刮去	guāqù	vc.	to scrape off
24	敷上药	敷上藥	fūshàng yào	vo.	to apply ointment
25	缝起来	縫起來	féngqǐlái	vc.	to stitch up
26	介意	介意	jièyì	v.	to mind
27	尖刀	尖刀	jiāndāo	n.	sharp knife
28	盆子	盆子	pénzi	n.	basin
29	位置	位置	wèizhì	n.	place

	SIMPLIFIED CHARACTERS	TRADITIONAL CHARACTERS	PINYIN	PART OF SPEECH	ENGLISH DEFINITION
30	悉悉	悉悉	*xīxī*	on.	(the sound of bleeding)
31	血	血	*xuè*	n.	blood
32	几乎	幾乎	*jīhū*	adv.	almost
33	装满	裝滿	*zhuāngmǎn*	vc.	to completely fill
34	情景	情景	*qíngjǐng*	n.	scene, sight
35	异常	異常	*yìcháng*	adj.	abnormal
36	勇敢无畏	勇敢無畏	*yǒnggǎn wúwèi*	adj.	courageous, fearless

Questions

1

Which of the following statements about Guan Gong is not true?

A. He is known as the Sage of Culture.

B. He is known as the Sage of War.

C. He was a famous general during the Three Kingdoms period.

D. He is admired for his bravery and nobility to this day.

2

When Guan Gong was struck with a poisoned arrow,

A. his soldiers urged him to stay with them for protection.

B. he treated the wound himself and refused to see a doctor.

C. his soldiers treated his wound immediately.

D. he refused to leave the battlefield for treatment.

3

Guan Gong played chess in order to

A. keep his mind off the pain from his wound.

B. challenge his soldiers' strategy-making skills.

C. keep himself entertained during treatment.

D. challenge his own strategy-making skills.

4 In order to treat Guan Gong's wound, the doctor needed to

A. stitch the wound and feed him an antidote.

B. scrape the poison off the bone and apply ointment.

C. apply ointment and bandage the wound.

D. scrape the poison off the bone and feed him an antidote.

5 What did Guan Gong do during the operation?

A. He shared a meal with the doctor.

B. He played chess with the doctor.

C. He ate, drank, and played chess.

D. He laughed hysterically through the pain.

DISCUSSION

1. 人们为什么都崇拜关公？
   人們為什麼都崇拜關公？

2. 为什么说关公是真正的大将军？
   為什麼說關公是真正的大將軍？

3. What do you think makes a great leader? Does Guan Gong fit your description?

4. Do leaders in today's world match your description of a great leader? How are they similar or different?

17

Mu Guiying, the Commander-in-Chief

穆桂英挂帅
穆桂英掛帥

Mù Guìyīng guàshuài

穆桂英是中国宋朝时期的女将军，也是中国人心目中的女英雄。穆桂英虽然是个女人，可是像男人一样，为了国家带兵打仗。她五十三岁那年，还当了主帅，带领军队，打败了敌人，保卫了国家。

传说穆桂英出生的时候，屋子里充满奇特的香味，持续了很长时间。当时正好是八月中秋，桂花开放的时候，所以爸爸妈妈给她起名叫桂英。穆桂英从小长得很可爱，聪明伶俐，人人喜爱。她跟着父亲和师父学武艺，常常一学就会。穆桂英十五、六岁时，就武艺精通，成熟可靠。她的父亲把管理山寨的任务交给她，让她当寨主。穆桂英当了寨主后，把山寨管理得井井有条，受到大家的拥护。

穆桂英是中國宋朝時期的女將軍，也是中國人心目中的女英雄。穆桂英雖然是個女人，可是像男人一樣，為了國家帶兵打仗。她五十三歲那年，還當了主帥，帶領軍隊，打敗了敵人，保衛了國家。

傳說穆桂英出生的時候，屋子裡充滿奇特的香味，持續了很長時間。當時正好是八月中秋，桂花開放的時候，所以爸爸媽媽給她起名叫桂英。穆桂英從小長得很可愛，聰明伶俐，人人喜愛。她跟著父親和師父學武藝，常常一學就會。穆桂英十五、六歲時，就武藝精通，成熟可靠。她的父親把管理山寨的任務交給她，讓她當寨主。穆桂英當了寨主後，把山寨管理得井井有條，受到大家的擁護。

当时北方的辽国常常侵犯宋朝。当时宋朝的大将军姓杨，他们家有八个男将军，中国人叫他们杨家将。穆桂英嫁到杨家以后，也跟杨家将一起带兵打仗。由于穆桂英有勇有谋，成了挂帅的女将军。多年的战争中，杨家将死的死，伤的伤，最后只剩了一些女人，叫杨门女将。这些女将由穆桂英带领，继续带兵打仗。但是当他们把敌人打败以后，当时的皇帝却解除了他们的兵权，命令他们回家当农民。

京城震动，乱作一团

二十多年过去了，辽国得知穆桂英早已不带兵打仗了，杨家将也老的老，死的死，就再次侵犯宋朝。辽军一连打了几个胜仗，快要拿下京城了。消息传来，京城震动，乱作一团，没有人敢领兵抗敌。皇帝急得没有办法，只好又要穆桂英当主帅。这一年，

穆桂英全身披掛，威風凜凜

當時北方的遼國常常侵犯宋朝。當時宋朝的大將軍姓楊，他們家有八個男將軍，中國人叫他們楊家將。穆桂英嫁到楊家以後，也跟楊家將一起帶兵打仗。由於穆桂英有勇有謀，成了掛帥的女將軍。多年的戰爭中，楊家將死的死，傷的傷，最後只剩了一些女人，叫楊門女將。這些女將由穆桂英帶領，繼續帶兵打仗。但是當他們把敵人打敗以後，當時的皇帝卻解除了他們的兵權，命令他們回家當農民。

二十多年過去了，遼國得知穆桂英早已不帶兵打仗了，楊家將也老的老，死的死，就再次侵犯宋朝。遼軍一連打了幾個勝仗，快要拿下京城了。消息傳來，京城震動，亂作一團，沒有人敢領兵抗敵。皇帝急得沒有辦法，只好又要穆桂英當穆桂英已经五十三岁了，她觉得自己年岁大了，加上她一直对皇帝和他的谋臣不满，所以不愿意挂帅。她打算向皇帝推辞，但是考虑到国家的安危，又改变了主意，同意挂帅出征。

出征那天，穆桂英全身披挂，威风凛凛。她的丈夫跟她一起带领大队人马，前往边关。经过激烈的战斗，他们打败了强大的敌人，保卫了国家，让老百姓过上快乐的日子。

主帥。這一年，<u>穆桂英</u>已經五十三歲了，她覺得自己年歲大了，加上她一直對皇帝和他的謀臣不滿，所以不願意掛帥。她打算向皇帝推辭，但是考慮到國家的安危，又改變了主意，同意掛帥出征。

出征那天，<u>穆桂英</u>全身披掛，威風凜凜。她的丈夫跟她一起帶領大隊人馬，前往邊關。經過激烈的戰斗，他們打敗了強大的敵人，保衛了國家，讓老百姓過上快樂的日子。

Vocabulary List

	SIMPLIFIED CHARACTERS	TRADITIONAL CHARACTERS	PINYIN	PART OF SPEECH	ENGLISH DEFINITION
1	挂帅	掛帥	guà shuài	vo.	to assume command/leadership (of a large army)
2	宋朝	宋朝	Sòngcháo	pn.	Song dynasty
3	主帅	主帥	zhǔshuài	n.	commander-in-chief
4	奇特	奇特	qítè	adj.	peculiar
5	香味	香味	xiāngwèi	n.	sweet smell, fragrance
6	持续	持續	chíxù	v.	to continue
7	桂花	桂花	guìhuā	n.	osmanthus flower
8	伶俐	伶俐	línglì	adj.	clever, bright
9	武艺精通	武藝精通	wǔyì jīngtōng	expr.	to have a good command of martial arts
10	成熟可靠	成熟可靠	chéngshú kěkào	adj.	mature and reliable
11	管理	管理	guǎnlǐ	v.	to manage
12	山寨	山寨	shānzhài	n.	fortified mountain village
13	任务	任務	rènwù	n.	task

	SIMPLIFIED CHARACTERS	TRADITIONAL CHARACTERS	PINYIN	PART OF SPEECH	ENGLISH DEFINITION
14	寨主	寨主	*zhàizhǔ*	n.	chief
15	井井有条	井井有條	*jǐngjǐng yǒutiáo*	expr.	in perfect order
16	拥护	擁護	*yōnghù*	v./n.	to support, to uphold; support
17	辽国	遼國	*Liáoguó*	pn.	state of Liao
18	侵犯	侵犯	*qīnfàn*	v.	to invade
19	杨家将	楊家將	*Yángjiā jiàng*	pn.	Generals of the Yang Family
20	嫁	嫁	*jià*	v.	(of a woman) to marry
21	有勇有谋	有勇有謀	*yǒuyǒng yǒumóu*	adj.	brave and resourceful
22	解除	解除	*jiěchú*	v.	to remove
23	兵权	兵權	*bīngquán*	n.	military leadership
24	命令	命令	*mìnglìng*	v.	to order
25	京城	京城	*jīngchéng*	n.	capital city
26	震动	震動	*zhèndòng*	vc.	to shake, to shock
27	乱作一团	亂作一團	*luànzuò yītuán*	adj.	chaotic, in great confusion
28	敢	敢	*gǎn*	v.	to dare

	SIMPLIFIED CHARACTERS	TRADITIONAL CHARACTERS	PINYIN	PART OF SPEECH	ENGLISH DEFINITION
29	不满	不滿	*bùmǎn*	adj.	dissatisfied, unhappy
30	推辞	推辭	*tuīcí*	v.	to decline (an appointment or invitation)
31	考虑	考慮	*kǎolǜ*	v.	to consider
32	安危	安危	*ānwēi*	n.	safety and danger
33	改变主意	改變主意	*gǎibiàn zhǔyì*	vo.	to change one's mind
34	出征	出征	*chūzhēng*	v.	to go out to battle
35	全身披挂	全身披掛	*quánshēn pīguà*	expr.	to be covered in armor
36	威风凛凛	威風凜凜	*wēifēnglǐnlǐn*	adj.	majestic-looking, awe-inspiring
37	边关	邊關	*biānguān*	n.	border station
38	激烈	激烈	*jīliè*	adj.	fierce

Questions

1 What was unique about Mu Guiying?

A. She was born with superhuman strength.

B. When she was born, the room filled with a peculiar smell.

C. She was born with the knowledge of a commander.

D. When she was born, the room filled with a continuous beam of light.

2 As Mu Guiying grew into a mature and reliable young woman, her father

A. began teaching her martial arts.

B. gave her all of his responsibilities as commander.

C. co-managed the mountain village with her.

D. gave her the responsibility of managing the mountain village.

3 Which of the following did not happen while Mu Guiying fought alongside the Yang army?

A. She took command above the eight male generals of the Yang family.

B. She headed the Women Generals of the Yang Family.

C. She took command when all the male generals were injured or killed.

D. Her position of military leadership was revoked by the emperor.

DISCUSSION

1. 穆桂英为什么是中国人心目中的女英雄?

   穆桂英為什麼是中國人心目中的女英雄?

2. 穆桂英为什么在五十三岁的时候，还要挂帅出征?

   穆桂英為什麼在五十三歲的時候，還要掛帥出征?

3. How was Mu Guiying able to attain such power during the Song dynasty? Using resources online, find out how the social status of women changed during this time period.

4. Mu Guiying's story bears many similarities to the legend of Hua Mulan. Despite such similarities, what differences are there between these two prominent female figures and the times they lived in?

女英雄馮婉貞

女英雄馮婉貞

18

The Heroine Feng Wanzhen

女英雄冯婉贞
女英雄馮婉貞

Nǚ yīngxióng Féng Wǎnzhēn

在中国的清朝，英国法国联合起来打进了北京。他们到处放火抢劫，做了很多坏事。北京的老百姓纷纷团结起来，保卫自己的家乡。

北京西边有一个村子叫谢庄。谢庄的老百姓成立了自卫团，团长有个女儿叫<u>冯婉贞</u>，才十九岁。她长得聪明漂亮，精通武艺。有一天，她父亲远远看见来了一队英国兵，他赶快回到村子里，告诉自卫团敌人来了，赶快做好准备。英国兵在离村子还很远的时候就开始放枪，他们看见村子里没有动静，就大着胆子继续走。等敌人走近了，团长才喊了一声："打！"自卫团一起冲出来，对着敌人放枪，很快把敌人打跑了。

敌人被打跑了，大家都很高兴。<u>冯婉贞</u>却很担心，她说："敌人不会轻易放弃的，一定马上会来更多的人，用更强大的在中國的清朝，英國法國聯合起來打進了北京。他們到處放火搶劫，做了很多壞事。北京的老百姓紛紛團結起來，保衛自己的家鄉。

北京西邊有一個村子叫謝莊。謝莊的老百姓成立了自衛團，團長有個女兒叫馮婉貞，才十九歲。她長得聰明漂亮，精通武藝。有一天，她父親遠遠看見來了一隊英國兵，他趕快回到村子裡，告訴自衛團敵人來了，趕快做好準備。英國兵在離村子還很遠的時候就開始放槍，他們看見村子裡沒有動靜，就大著膽子繼續走。等敵人走近了，團長才喊了一聲："打！"自衛團一起衝出來，對著敵人放槍，很快把敵人打跑了。

敵人被打跑了，大家都很高興。馮婉貞卻很擔心，她說："敵人不會輕易放棄的，一定馬上會來更多的人，用更強大的武器來

敌人纷纷败退

武器来报仇。咱们的枪很少，又没有大炮，要是敌人拉着大炮来打我们，咱们村就会被毁了！咱们得想个办法。"大家问："你有什么办法吗？"

冯婉贞说："谢庄周围都是平原，我们应该用我们的长处，去攻打敌人的短处。我们拿着刀，带着盾，跟敌人近距离搏斗，一定能把敌人打败。"他的父亲不同意她的想法，也不希望女孩子多说话。

冯婉贞觉得只有这个办法才能打败敌人，保卫自己的村子。她召集了村子里会武术的年轻人，要他们都穿着黑色的衣服，拿着雪亮的钢刀，埋伏在村子附近的一片森林里。没有多久，敌人果然来了，一共有六百多人。冯婉贞一声令下，带领大家飞快地向敌人冲过去，敌人没有准备，枪炮来不及发射。很快，敌人死伤了一百多，他们扔下枪炮，纷纷败退，一起逃跑了。

谢庄从此平安无事，村民们过着快乐的日子。他们都很感激冯婉贞，称她为"女英雄"。

報仇。咱們的槍很少，又沒有大炮，要是敵人拉著大炮來打我們，咱們村就會被毀了！咱們得想個辦法。"大家問："你有什麼辦法嗎？"

馮婉貞說："謝莊周圍都是平原，我們應該用我們的長處，去攻打敵人的短處。我們拿著刀，帶著盾，跟敵人近距離搏鬥，一定能把敵人打敗。"他的父親不同意她的想法，也不希望女孩子多說話。

馮婉貞覺得只有這個辦法才能打敗敵人，保衛自己的村子。她召集了村子裡會武術的年輕人，要他們都穿著黑色的衣服，拿著雪亮的鋼刀，埋伏在村子附近的一片森林裡。沒有多久，敵人果然來了，一共有六百多人。馮婉貞一聲令下，帶領大家飛快地向敵人沖過去，敵人沒有準備，槍炮來不及發射。很快，敵人死傷了一百多，他們扔下槍炮，紛紛敗退，一起逃跑了。

謝莊從此平安無事，村民們過著快樂的日子。他們都很感激馮婉貞，稱她為"女英雄"。

Vocabulary List

	SIMPLIFIED CHARACTERS	TRADITIONAL CHARACTERS	PINYIN	PART OF SPEECH	ENGLISH DEFINITION
1	清朝	清朝	*Qīngcháo*	pn.	Qing dynasty
2	放火	放火	*fàng huǒ*	vo.	to set on fire
3	抢劫	搶劫	*qiǎngjié*	v.	to rob
4	保卫	保衛	*bǎowèi*	v.	to defend
5	谢庄	謝莊	*Xièzhuāng*	pn.	Xie village
6	自卫团	自衛團	*zìwèituán*	n.	self-defense corps
7	放枪	放槍	*fàng qiāng*	vo.	to fire a gun
8	动静	動靜	*dòngjing*	n.	movement, activity
9	大着胆子	大著膽子	*dàzhe dǎnzi*	vo.	to be brave

	SIMPLIFIED CHARACTERS	TRADITIONAL CHARACTERS	PINYIN	PART OF SPEECH	ENGLISH DEFINITION
10	团长	團長	*tuánzhǎng*	n.	regimental commander
11	轻易	輕易	*qīngyì*	adv.	easily
12	放弃	放棄	*fàngqì*	v.	to give up
13	大炮	大炮	*dàpào*	n.	artillery
14	毁	毀	*huǐ*	v.	to destroy
15	周围	周圍	*zhōuwéi*	n.	surroundings
16	平原	平原	*píngyuán*	n.	field, plain
17	长处	長處	*chángchù*	n.	strong points
18	短处	短處	*duǎnchù*	n.	shortcomings

19	搏斗	搏鬥	*bódòu*	v.	to fight, to wrestle
20	召集	召集	*zhàojí*	v.	to call together
21	雪亮	雪亮	*xuěliàng*	adj.	shiny
22	钢	鋼	*gāng*	n.	steel
23	埋伏	埋伏	*máifú*	v.	to ambush
24	果然	果然	*guǒrán*	adv.	as expected
25	带领	帶領	*dàilǐng*	v.	to lead
26	发射	發射	*fāshè*	v.	to shoot, to fire
27	扔下	扔下	*rēngxià*	vc.	to abandon
28	平安无事	平安無事	*píng'ānwúshì*	expr.	safe and sound

Questions

1 Feng Wanzhen's strategy to defeat the British and French troops was to

A. take advantage of the plains around the village and hide.

B. fight from a distance to prevent harm to the village.

C. take advantage of the plains around the village and fight at close range.

D. steal and use artillery instead of fighting with knives and shields.

2 How did Feng Wanzhen's father respond to her strategy?

A. He disagreed and did not allow her to fight.

B. He disagreed and insisted that girls should not talk too much.

C. He agreed with her strategy, but did not allow her to fight.

D. He agreed with her strategy and joined her in the fight.

3 In executing her plan, which of the following did Feng Wanzhen not do?

A. She called together the young martial artists of the village.

B. She had her army wear black and hide in the forest.

C. She and her father led a surprise attack against the enemy.

D. She led an attack before the enemy could return fire.

1. 北京的老百姓为什么要成立自卫团？
   北京的老百姓為什麼要成立自衛團？

2. <u>冯婉贞</u>用什么办法保护了自己的村子？
   <u>馮婉貞</u>用什麼辦法保衛了自己的村子？

3. Why did the Opium Wars break out? Using resources online, find out why France and Britain invaded Beijing during the Qing dynasty.

V

Myths and Fantasies

第五章 神话故事

第五章 神話故事

Chinese myths, much like those in other cultures, were once considered historical record. Many Chinese myths originated long before being written down, but were later recorded in ancient texts containing a wealth of historical and cultural information. While the lines between history and mythology are often blurred in these traditions, they reflect the important historical influences and cultural values of Chinese civilization. The myth of Shen Nong, for example, reveals the origins of Chinese medicine, a discipline that shares many principles and concepts with other facets of Chinese culture and philosophy. The story of Emperor Shun's rise to power reflects Confucian values such as filial piety. In other stories in this unit, you will also read about the Eight Immortals, as well as Zhu Bajie, an important character in *Journey to the West*, who follows a Buddhist monk's pilgrimage to India to obtain sacred texts.

19

Shen Nong Tastes Hundreds of Herbs

神农尝百草

神農嘗百草

Shén Nóng cháng bǎi cǎo

传说神农是发明中国农事和医药的人。

在神农以前，五谷粮食和杂草长在一起，谁也不知道哪些是粮食，哪些是杂草。也就是说他们不知道哪些可以吃，哪些不可以吃。

后来瘟疫开始流行，人们又不知道怎样治疗疾病，他们不知道哪些花草可以治病，哪些不可以治病，因此很多人病死了。神农看在眼里，疼在心头。他要想出办法，为人们找到食物和治病的药。为了解决这两个问题，神农决定到大山里面去亲口尝试各种花草。

他带着一些老百姓，向大山里走去。他们爬了很多山，走了很多路，直到看见茂盛的花草树木时才停下来。神农用鞭子抽打草木，直到打出汁液，然后亲口尝一尝，这样他就可以知道这些草木的性质和味道。

傳說神農是發明中國農事和醫藥的人。

在神農以前，五穀糧食和雜草長在一起，誰也不知道哪些是糧食，哪些是雜草。也就是說他們不知道哪些可以吃，哪些不可以吃。

後來瘟疫開始流行，人們又不知道怎樣治療疾病，他們不知道哪些花草可以治病，哪些不可以治病，因此很多人病死了。神農看在眼裡，疼在心頭。他要想出辦法，為人們找到食物和治病的藥。為了解決這兩個問題，神農決定到大山裡面去親口嘗試各種花草。

他帶著一些老百姓，向大山裡走去。他們爬了很多山，走了很多路，直到看見茂盛的花草樹木時才停下來。神農用鞭子抽打草木，直到打出汁液，然後親口嘗一嘗，這樣他就可以知道這些草木的性質和味道。

就这样，白天神农带着人们到山上去尝花草。晚上他生起柴火，借着火光把心得写下来。比如说，哪些草是苦的，哪些草是热的，哪些草是凉的，哪些能吃，哪些能治病，等等，他都写得清清楚楚。有时在一天之内，神农尝了七十多种花草，连续中毒几十次。

他发现了
三百六十五种草药

为了尝花草，神农走过了每一座山。终于，他分出了哪些是可以吃的，哪些是不可以吃的，哪些花草可以治病，哪些不可以治病。神农分出了麦、稻、谷子、豆子、高粱是能吃的，他叫老百姓把种子带回去，教人们怎么播种，怎么生产粮食。这就是后来的五谷粮食。

另外，神农也发现了三百六十五种草药，它们能治疗一百多种疾病。他按照记下来的心得，写成了一本书，为老百姓治病。这本书就這樣，白天神農帶著人們到山上去嘗花草。晚上他生起柴火，借著火光把心得寫下來。比如說，哪些草是苦的，哪些草是熱的，哪些草是涼的，哪些能吃，哪些能治病，等等，他都寫得清清楚楚。有時在一天之內，神農嘗了七十多種花草，連續中毒幾十次。

為了嘗花草，神農走過了每一座山。終於，他分出了哪些是可以吃的，哪些是不可以吃的，哪些花草可以治病，哪些不可以治病。神農分出了麥、稻、穀子、豆子、高粱是能吃的，他叫老百姓把種子帶回去，教人們怎麼播種，怎麼生產糧食。這就是後來的五穀糧食。

他為人們建立了
完整的醫藥基礎

就是《神农本草经》，它一共记载了上等药一百二十种，吃了不但可以治病，还可延年益寿；中等药一百二十种，吃了不但可以治病，还可以养性；下等药一百二十五种，吃了可以治病。

虽然神农已经为百姓解决了粮食和治病的问题，但是他还是持续不停地尝试各种花草。直到有一天，神农尝了一种叫"火焰子"的草，中毒而死。

神农牺牲了自己，为人们建立了完整的医药基础。可以说后来中国几千年的中药发展，都是建立在《神农本草经》的基础上的。因此，神农被称为中国的医药之祖，老百姓又叫他"药王菩萨"。

另外，神農也發現了三百六十五種草藥，它們能治療一百多種疾病。他按照記下來的心得，寫成了一本書，為老百姓治病。這本書就是《神農本草經》，它一共記載了上等藥一百二十種，吃了不但可以治病，還可延年益壽；中等藥一百二十種，吃了不但可以治病，還可以養性；下等藥一百二十五種，吃了可以治病。

雖然神農已經為百姓解決了糧食和治病的問題，但是他還是持續不停地嘗試各種花草。直到有一天，神農嘗了一種叫"火焰子"的草，中毒而死。

神農犧牲了自己，為人們建立了完整的醫藥基礎。可以說後來中國幾千年的中藥發展，都是建立在《神農本草經》的基礎上的。因此，神農被稱為中國的醫藥之祖，老百姓又叫他"藥王菩薩"。

Vocabulary List

	SIMPLIFIED CHARACTERS	TRADITIONAL CHARACTERS	PINYIN	PART OF SPEECH	ENGLISH DEFINITION
1	神农	神農	Shén Nóng	pn.	the Divine Farmer
2	发明	發明	fāmíng	v.	to discover
3	农事	農事	nóngshì	n.	farming, agricultural practice
4	五谷粮食	五穀糧食	wǔgǔ liángshi	n.	the five grains (rice, two kinds of millet, wheat, and beans)
5	杂草	雜草	zácǎo	n.	weeds
6	瘟疫	瘟疫	wēnyì	n.	plague, epidemic disease
7	流行	流行	liúxíng	adj./v.	prevalent; to spread
8	疾病	疾病	jíbìng	n.	disease
9	食物	食物	shíwù	n.	food
10	解决	解決	jiějué	v.	to solve
11	尝试	嘗試	chángshì	v.	to attempt, to try
12	茂盛	茂盛	màoshèng	adj.	flourishing
13	鞭子	鞭子	biānzi	n.	whip
14	抽打	抽打	chōudǎ	v.	to lash, to whip

shen nong tastes hundreds of herbs　神農嘗百草

	SIMPLIFIED CHARACTERS	TRADITIONAL CHARACTERS	PINYIN	PART OF SPEECH	ENGLISH DEFINITION
15	汁液	汁液	zhīyè	n.	juice
16	性质	性質	xìngzhì	n.	nature, quality
17	味道	味道	wèidào	n.	taste
18	心得	心得	xīndé	n.	knowledge gained, reflections
19	连续	連續	liánxù	adv.	continuously
20	中毒	中毒	zhòng dú	vo.	to be poisoned
21	麦	麥	mài	n.	wheat
22	稻	稻	dào	n.	rice paddy
23	谷子	穀子	gǔzi	n.	millet
24	豆子	豆子	dòuzi	n.	bean
25	高粱	高粱	gāoliang	n.	sorghum (a type of grain)
26	种子	種子	zhǒngzi	n.	seeds
27	播种	播種	bōzhòng	v.	to sow
28	草药	草藥	cǎoyào	n.	herbs
29	神农本草经	神農本草經	Shén Nóng Běncǎo Jīng	pn.	The Divine Farmer's Herb-Root Classic
30	延年益寿	延年益壽	yánnián yìshòu	expr.	to prolong life

	SIMPLIFIED CHARACTERS	TRADITIONAL CHARACTERS	PINYIN	PART OF SPEECH	ENGLISH DEFINITION
31	养性	養性	*yǎng xìng*	vo.	to cultivate oneself, to nourish oneself
32	持续不停	持續不停	*chíxù bùtíng*	v.	to continue without stopping
33	牺牲	犧牲	*xīshēng*	v.	to sacrifice
34	完整	完整	*wánzhěng*	adj.	entire, complete
35	医药基础	醫藥基礎	*yīyào jīchǔ*	n.	medicinal foundation
36	医药之祖	醫藥之祖	*yīyào zhīzǔ*	n.	the forefather of medicine
37	药王菩萨	藥王菩薩	*Yàowáng Púsà*	pn.	Bodhisattva of Medicine

Questions

1 Why were deaths so frequent in Shen Nong's time?

A. People were eating herbs that they did not know
   were poisonous.

B. An epidemic had broken out.

C. People were eating herbs that made their diseases worse.

D. Swine flu was beginning to spread.

2 For what purpose did Shen Nong use a whip?

A. To keep his subordinates in line.

B. To extract juice from plants in order to create a
   universal remedy.

C. To clear brush and find the most effective herbs.

D. To extract juice from plants in order to taste each one.

3 For what purpose did Shen Nong use fire at night?

A. To create a potion by boiling herbs together.

B. To cook meals for himself and his crew.

C. As a light source in order to take notes on
   each plant.

D. To boil drinking water for whenever he ate
   something poisonous.

4 According to Shen Nong's book, how many herbs can prolong life?

A. 365
B. 125
C. 120
D. 100

5 Even after he completed his book, Shen Nong continued tasting different herbs, and

A. prolonged his life for hundreds of years.
B. died from a plague.
C. discovered an herb of immortality.
D. died from eating a poisonous herb.

DISCUSSION

1. 神农为什么决定到大山里面去亲口尝试各种花草?

   神農為什麼決定到大山裡面去親口嘗試各種花草？

2. 神农是怎样发现五谷粮食的?

   神農是怎樣發現五穀糧食的？

3. Using resources online, research the basic principles of traditional Chinese medicine. For example, what are "hot" and "cold" foods? How do such principles connect or align with broader aspects of Chinese culture?

4. Continuing your research, pick a form of Chinese medicine or a particular medicinal herb that catches your interest. How is it used, and what is it used to treat?

20

The Story of Emperor Shun

舜帝的故事
舜帝的故事

Shùn Dì de gùshi

舜是传说中的五帝之一，他的母亲在他很小的时候就死了。后来，舜的父亲又结了婚，生了一个弟弟。不幸的是，舜的后母和弟弟一直不喜欢舜。有一次，他们叫舜去修理屋顶，等舜到了屋顶上，他们在下面放火。舜从屋顶上跳下去，幸运地逃脱了。还有一次，他们让舜去挖一口井，当舜在井里时，他们用土把井填起来。聪明的舜已经事先在井边挖了一个出口，他就从那个出口逃出来了。

可是，舜不但不怨恨他的后母和弟弟，而且对他们很好。舜这么孝敬父母，爱护弟弟，感动了很多人，连当时的皇帝尧也很感动，认为舜是个好青年。

后来尧帝老了，问谁能接替他，大家都推举舜。由于舜只是一个普通老百姓，尧就让自己的女儿去跟他结婚，并让自己的九个

舜是傳說中的五帝之一，他的母親在他很小的時候就死了。後來，舜的父親又結了婚，生了一個弟弟。不幸的是，舜的後母和弟弟一直不喜歡舜。有一次，他們叫舜去修理屋頂，等舜到了屋頂上，他們在下面放火。舜從屋頂上跳下去，幸運地逃脫了。還有一次，他們讓舜去挖一口井，當舜在井裡時，他們用土把井填起來。聰明的舜已經事先在井邊挖了一個出口，他就從那個出口逃出來了。

可是，舜不但不怨恨他的後母和弟弟，而且對他們很好。舜這麼孝敬父母，愛護弟弟，感動了很多人，連當時的皇帝堯也很感動，認為舜是個好青年。

後來堯帝老了，問誰能接替他，大家都推舉舜。由於舜只是一個普通老百姓，堯就讓自己的女兒去跟他結婚，並讓自己

儿子和舜一起工作。结果尧的女儿跟舜结婚以后，变得很负责任；尧的儿子跟舜一起工作以后，也都变得更加谦虚谨慎。还有，不管舜到了哪里，那里的人都会变得更加善良。舜每到一个地方，人们都会热烈欢迎他。

尧看到舜不但对家里的人那么好，而且能感动很多别的人，所以他对舜的印象特别好，让舜管理很多事务，并让舜宣扬伦理道德。同时，尧又让舜进入山林，遇上暴风雷雨，舜也没有迷路。尧认为舜聪明，有道德，所以决定让他接替，最后舜当上了皇帝。

后来舜自己年老时，也向尧学习，将皇帝的位子让给了治水有功的大禹。

的九個兒子和舜一起工作。結果堯的女兒跟舜結婚以後，變得很負責任；堯的兒子跟舜一起工作以後，也都變得更加謙虛謹慎。還有，不管舜到了哪裡，那裡的人都會變得更加善良。舜每到一個地方，人們都會熱烈歡迎他。

堯看到舜不但對家裡的人那麼好，而且能感動很多別的人，所以他對舜的印象特別好，讓舜管理很多事務，並讓舜宣揚倫理道德。同時，堯又讓舜進入山林，遇上暴風雷雨，舜也沒有迷路。堯認為舜聰明，有道德，所以決定讓他接替，最後舜當上了皇帝。

後來舜自己年老時，也向堯學習，將皇帝的位子讓給了治水有功的大禹。

Vocabulary List

	SIMPLIFIED CHARACTERS	TRADITIONAL CHARACTERS	PINYIN	PART OF SPEECH	ENGLISH DEFINITION
1	不幸	不幸	*bùxìng*	adj.	unfortunate
2	后母	後母	*hòumǔ*	n.	stepmother
3	修理	修理	*xiūlǐ*	v.	to repair
4	屋顶	屋頂	*wūdǐng*	n.	roof
5	幸运地	幸運地	*xìngyùn de*	adv.	fortunately, luckily
6	逃脱	逃脱	*táotuō*	v.	to escape
7	挖	挖	*wā*	v.	to dig
8	填	填	*tián*	v.	to fill up
9	事先	事先	*shìxiān*	adv.	beforehand
10	怨恨	怨恨	*yuànhèn*	v.	to hate, to have a grudge against
11	孝敬	孝敬	*xiàojìng*	v.	to be filial and respectful

	SIMPLIFIED CHARACTERS	TRADITIONAL CHARACTERS	PINYIN	PART OF SPEECH	ENGLISH DEFINITION
12	爱护	愛護	àihù	v.	to take good care of, to cherish
13	尧帝	堯帝	Yáo Dì	pn.	Emperor Yao
14	接替	接替	jiētì	v.	to succeed
15	推举	推舉	tuījǔ	v.	to choose
16	负责任	負責任	fù zérèn	vo.	to take responsibility
17	谦虚谨慎	謙虛謹慎	qiānxū jǐnshèn	adj.	modest and prudent
18	不管	不管	bù guǎn	conj.	regardless of
19	更加	更加	gèngjiā	adv.	more
20	善良	善良	shànliáng	adj.	good and kind, kindhearted
21	热烈	熱烈	rèliè	adj./adv.	enthusiastic; entlausiastically

	SIMPLIFIED CHARACTERS	TRADITIONAL CHARACTERS	PINYIN	PART OF SPEECH	ENGLISH DEFINITION
22	印象	印象	yìnxiàng	n.	impression
23	事务	事務	shìwù	n.	affairs, matters, work
24	宣扬	宣揚	xuānyáng	v.	to promote, to propagate
25	伦理道德	倫理道德	lúnlǐ dàodé	n.	ethics and morals
26	暴风雷雨	暴風雷雨	bàofēng léiyǔ	expr.	violent winds and thunderstorms
27	迷路	迷路	mí lù	vo.	to lose one's way
28	位子	位子	wèizi	n.	place, seat
29	让给	讓給	rànggěi	v.	to offer
30	有功的	有功的	yǒugōng de	adj.	meritorious

1 What did Shun not do when his brother and stepmother tried to trap him?

A. He resented them for trying to hurt him.

B. He jumped down from the roof of a burning building.

C. He took care of his brother and was respectful towards his stepmother.

D. He dug himself an escape tunnel from the bottom of a well.

2 What influence did Shun have on Emperor Yao's family?

A. The emperor's daughter became very dependent on Shun.

B. The emperor's sons became very dependent on Shun.

C. The emperor's daughter became very modest and prudent.

D. The emperor's sons became very modest and prudent.

3 In what way did Shun follow in Emperor Yao's footsteps?

A. He entered a forest during a storm without getting lost.

B. He escaped from the bottom of a well by digging an exit tunnel.

C. He passed the emperor's throne on to Da Yu.

D. He helped his brother and stepmother fix their roof.

DISCUSSION

1. 舜是怎样孝敬父母爱护弟弟的?
   舜是怎樣孝敬父母愛護弟弟的？

2. 为什么舜每到一个地方人们都会热烈
   欢迎他?
   為什麼舜每到一個地方人們都會熱烈
   歡迎他？

3. Why do you think Shun was revered and highly regarded? Look back in the text and see how many Confucian values you can identify.

4. Why do you think Shun chose Da Yu as the next emperor? You may refer to your previous knowledge about Da Yu from *Tales and Traditions*, Volume 1, or to information online. Compared with how kings were chosen in other civilizations, how was the selection of Da Yu different?

海上守护神林默娘

海上守護神林默娘

21

Lin Moniang, Goddess of the Sea

海上守护神林默娘
海上守護神林默娘

Hǎishàng shǒuhù shén Lín Mòniáng

古时候，有一位老人叫林愿，他常常帮助别人，所以大家都很喜欢他。林愿与妻子王氏已经有一个儿子和五个女儿，但是儿子从小就一直生病，所以他们天天向观音菩萨祷告，希望能再生一个儿子。

有一天晚上，王氏梦见观音菩萨给她一片药，王氏吃下去，早上醒来就发现自己怀孕了。生孩子的那一天，只见一道红光从天上射进屋里，屋里充满异香，王氏生下一个女儿。这个女孩从出生到满月没哭过一声，所以林愿就给她起名叫默娘，意思是沉默的姑娘。

默娘从小就很聪明，读过的书都能记住。默娘十六岁时，有一天在外面玩儿，突然来了一位神仙。神仙交给默娘一道法力，从此默娘学得一身法术。她决心终生不嫁人，以便更好地帮助老百姓。她专心

<big>古</big>時候，有一位老人叫林願，他常常幫助別人，所以大家都很喜歡他。林願與妻子王氏已經有一個兒子和五個女兒，但是兒子從小就一直生病，所以他們天天向觀音菩薩禱告，希望能再生一個兒子。

有一天晚上，王氏夢見觀音菩薩給她一片藥，王氏吃下去，早上醒來就發現自己懷孕了。生孩子的那一天，只見一道紅光從天上射進屋裡，屋裡充滿異香，王氏生下一個女兒。這個女孩從出生到滿月沒哭過一聲，所以林願就給她起名叫默娘，意思是沉默的姑娘。

默娘從小就很聰明，讀過的書都能記住。默娘十六歲時，有一天在外面玩兒，突然來了一位神仙。神仙交給默娘一道法力，從此默娘學得一身法術。她決心

研究医学，为人治病。她对人热心，谁遇到困难，都去请她帮忙。当时，瘟疫流行，默娘想了很多办法来抢救乡民，她看过的病人，都很快就好了，所以大家都很感激她。

除了替人治病以外，默娘还常常在海上守护船只。暴风雨中，人们看见一个穿红衣服的女孩子，手里提着一只大红灯笼，把遇难的人从海里救出来，并指引他们回家。老百姓很感激默娘，为她修建了庙宇，称她为海上女神，常常朝拜。而默娘也常常显灵，穿着红衣服，拿着大灯笼，保护着海上的船只。

終生不嫁人，以便更好地幫助老百姓。她專心研究醫學，為人治病。她對人熱心，誰遇到困難，都去請她幫忙。當時，瘟疫流行，默娘想了很多辦法來搶救鄉民，她看過的病人，都很快就好了，所以大家都很感激她。

除了替人治病以外，默娘還常常在海上守護船隻。暴風雨中，人們看見一個穿紅衣服的女孩子，手裡提著一隻大紅燈籠，把遇難的人從海裡救出來，並指引他們回家。老百姓很感激默娘，為她修建了廟宇，稱她為海上女神，常常朝拜。而默娘也常常顯靈，穿著紅衣服，拿著大燈籠，保護著海上的船隻。

Vocabulary List

	SIMPLIFIED CHARACTERS	TRADITIONAL CHARACTERS	PINYIN	PART OF SPEECH	ENGLISH DEFINITION
1	林愿	林願	*Lín Yuàn*	pn.	(name of a person)
2	祷告	禱告	*dǎogào*	v.	to pray
3	射进	射進	*shèjìn*	vc.	to shoot into
4	异香	異香	*yìxiāng*	n.	rare fragrance
5	沉默	沉默	*chénmò*	adj.	silent
6	交给	交給	*jiāogěi*	vc.	to hand over
7	法力	法力	*fǎlì*	n.	supernatural power
8	法术	法術	*fǎshù*	n.	magic arts
9	决心	決心	*juéxīn*	vo.	to make up one's mind
10	终生	終生	*zhōngshēng*	n.	all one's life
11	以便	以便	*yǐbiàn*	conj.	so that
12	研究	研究	*yánjiū*	v.	to study, to research
13	抢救	搶救	*qiǎngjiù*	v.	to rescue, to rush to save
14	乡民	鄉民	*xiāngmín*	n.	villager
15	提	提	*tí*	v.	to carry, to lift
16	指引	指引	*zhǐyǐn*	v.	to guide
17	庙宇	廟宇	*miàoyǔ*	n.	temple

	SIMPLIFIED CHARACTERS	TRADITIONAL CHARACTERS	PINYIN	PART OF SPEECH	ENGLISH DEFINITION
18	海上女神	海上女神	*Hǎishàng Nǚshén*	pn.	Goddess of the Sea
19	朝拜	朝拜	*cháobài*	v.	to worship
20	显灵	顯靈	*xiǎn líng*	vo.	to make one's power or presence felt

Questions

1 Why was Lin Moniang special?

A. A beam of light shot into the room on the day of her birth.

B. When she was born, the room filled with a rare fragrance.

C. She did not cry for the first month of her life.

D. All of the above.

2 Why did Lin Yuan give his daughter the name Moniang?

A. She cried for the first month of her life.

B. She did not cry for the first month of her life.

C. She had supernatural powers.

D. She was very warmhearted and intelligent.

3 Which of the following statements about Lin Moniang is untrue?

A. She did not speak a word her entire life.

B. She studied medicine and healed her fellow villagers.

C. She wore red clothing and held a red lantern.

D. She protected boats at sea.

1. 王氏是怎样怀上林默娘的？
   王氏是怎樣懷上林默娘的？

2. 为什么林默娘决心终生不嫁人？
   為什麼林默娘決心終生不嫁人？

3. Using resources online, research why and how Lin Moniang is worshipped in coastal areas throughout Asia. Who is worshipped in coastal areas in other cultural traditions? How do other worship practices compare to those for Lin Moniang?

22

The Eight Immortals Cross the Sea

八仙过海
八仙過海

Bā Xiān guò hǎi

八仙是中国的众多神仙中影响最大的。他们分别是汉钟离、张果老、铁拐李、韩湘子、曹国舅、吕洞宾、蓝采和，还有何仙姑。这八位神仙各有道术，法力无边，而且有很多有趣的故事。八仙过海便是他们最有趣的故事之一。

传说有一次，八仙去参加一个聚会，在那儿喝了很多酒。出来的时候，他们都喝醉了。远远地，他们看见了波涛汹涌的东海，都想赶快过去，可是没有船。这时，吕洞宾建议大家不要坐船，每个人想出自己的办法来过海。大家都同意了。

铁拐李第一个过海。他把手里的拐杖抛进东海，拐杖马上浮在水面上，铁拐李站在上面，一下子就到了对岸。接着汉钟离将他的拂尘抛进水中，站在拂尘上，也稳当地过了东海。轮到张果老时，只见他将他的纸驴八仙是中國的眾多神仙中影響最大的。他們分別是漢鐘離、張果老、鐵拐李、韓湘子、曹國舅、呂洞賓、藍采和，還有何仙姑。這八位神仙各有道術，法力無邊，而且有很多有趣的故事。八仙過海便是他們最有趣的故事之一。

傳說有一次，八仙去參加一個聚會，在那兒喝了很多酒。出來的時候，他們都喝醉了。遠遠地，他們看見了波濤洶湧的東海，都想趕快過去，可是沒有船。這時，呂洞賓建議大家不要坐船，每個人想出自己的辦法來過海。大家都同意了。

鐵拐李第一個過海。他把手裡的拐杖拋進東海，拐杖馬上浮在水面上，鐵拐李站在上面，一下子就到了對岸。接著漢鐘離將他的拂塵拋進水中，站在拂塵上，也穩當地

投进海中，纸驴马上变成了一头真正的驴，张果老骑在它的背上，向大家挥挥手，一会儿也到了对岸。何仙姑将荷花往水中一抛，站在荷花上面，也很快漂到了对岸。然后，吕洞宾用他的箫管，韩湘子用他的花篮，蓝采和用他的大拍板，曹国舅用他的玉板，一个一个都到了对岸。

八位神仙借助自己的宝物大显神通，顺利渡过东海，这就是人们常说的"八仙过海，各显神通"。后来人们常常用这个成语来比喻做事各有各的一套办法，或者比喻各自拿出自己的本领来互相比赛。

過了東海。輪到張果老時，只見他將他的紙驢投進海中，紙驢馬上變成了一頭真正的驢，張果老騎在它的背上，向大家揮揮手，一會兒也到了對岸。何仙姑將荷花往水中一拋，站在荷花上面，也很快漂到了對岸。然後，呂洞賓用他的簫管，韓湘子用他的花籃，藍采和用他的大拍板，曹國舅用他的玉板，一個一個都到了對岸。

八位神仙借助自己的寶物大顯神通，順利渡過東海，這就是人們常說的＂八仙過海，各顯神通＂。後來人們常常用這個成語來比喻做事各有各的一套辦法，或者比喻各自拿出自己的本領來互相比賽。

Vocabulary List

	SIMPLIFIED CHARACTERS	TRADITIONAL CHARACTERS	PINYIN	PART OF SPEECH	ENGLISH DEFINITION
1	影响	影響	yǐngxiǎng	n.	influence
2	分别	分別	fēnbié	adv.	respectively
3	汉钟离	漢鐘離	Hàn Zhōnglí	pn.	(name of an immortal)
4	张果老	張果老	Zhāng Guǒlǎo	pn.	(name of an immortal)
5	铁拐李	鐵拐李	Tiě Guǎilǐ	pn.	(name of an immortal)
6	韩湘子	韓湘子	Hán Xiāngzǐ	pn.	(name of an immortal)
7	曹国舅	曹國舅	Cáo Guójiù	pn.	(name of an immortal)
8	吕洞宾	呂洞賓	Lǚ Dòngbīn	pn.	(name of an immortal)
9	蓝采和	藍采和	Lán Cǎihé	pn.	(name of an immortal)
10	何仙姑	何仙姑	Hé Xiāngū	pn.	(name of an immortal)
11	道术	道術	dàoshù	n.	Taoist arts
12	法力无边	法力無邊	fǎlì wúbiān	expr.	boundless power

	SIMPLIFIED CHARACTERS	TRADITIONAL CHARACTERS	PINYIN	PART OF SPEECH	ENGLISH DEFINITION
13	喝醉	喝醉	*hēzuì*	vc.	to be drunk
14	波涛汹涌	波濤洶湧	*bōtāo xiōngyǒng*	expr.	surging waves
15	拐杖	拐杖	*guǎizhàng*	n.	cane
16	抛进	抛進	*pāojìn*	vc.	to toss in
17	浮	浮	*fú*	v.	to float
18	对岸	對岸	*duì'àn*	n.	the opposite shore
19	拂尘	拂塵	*fúchén*	n.	horsetail whisk (a weapon)
20	稳当	穩當	*wěndang*	adj.	secure, stable
21	纸驴	紙驢	*zhǐlǘ*	n.	paper donkey
22	投进	投進	*tóujìn*	vc.	to throw in
23	挥挥手	揮揮手	*huīhui shǒu*	vo.	to wave one's hand
24	荷花	荷花	*héhuā*	n.	lotus

	SIMPLIFIED CHARACTERS	TRADITIONAL CHARACTERS	PINYIN	PART OF SPEECH	ENGLISH DEFINITION
25	箫管	簫管	*xiāoguǎn*	n.	flute
26	花篮	花籃	*huālán*	n.	flower basket
27	拍板	拍板	*pāibǎn*	n.	clappers
28	玉板	玉板	*yùbǎn*	n.	jade clappers
29	借助	借助	*jièzhù*	vc.	to draw support from
30	宝物	寶物	*bǎowù*	n.	treasure
31	大显神通	大顯神通	*dàxiǎn shéntōng*	expr.	to show or display one's magical powers
32	顺利	順利	*shùnlì*	adj.	smooth, successful
33	渡过	渡過	*dùguò*	v.	to cross
34	本领	本領	*běnlǐng*	n.	skill, ability

Questions

1 Which of the eight immortals crossed the sea with a paper donkey?

A. Han Zhongli

B. Zhang Guolao

C. Tie Guaili

D. Han Xiangzi

2 Which of the eight immortals used musical instruments to cross the sea?

A. Lü Dongbin, Tie Guaili, and Han Zhongli

B. Zhang Guolao and He Xiangu

C. Lü Dongbin, Lan Caihe, and Cao Guojiu

D. Han Xiangzi, Lan Caihe, and Cao Guojiu

3 The idiom that comes from this story is used to describe

A. people using their own unique skills to complete a task or compete with one another.

B. the dangers of showing off in order to outdo others.

C. people who are talented and like to show off.

D. what not to try at home without supervision.

1. 八仙是怎么聚在一起的？
   八仙是怎麼聚在一起的？

2. 他们是怎么过海的？
   他們是怎麼過海的？

3. Which of the eight immortals would you want to be and why? Describe the character of your choice and discuss the pros and cons with a partner.

23

Zhu Bajie Takes a Wife

猪八戒娶亲
豬八戒娶親

Zhū Bājiè qǔ qīn

猪八戒原来是天上玉皇大帝的元帅，统领十万天兵天将。可是有一次他在蟠桃会上喝醉了，调戏了仙女嫦娥，被赶出天界，到人间投胎。不幸的是，他投错了胎，投到一只大母猪的肚子里去了，结果变成了一头猪，所以姓猪，起名叫八戒。大家都叫他猪八戒。

猪八戒武艺高强，又懂得变身术。有一天他来到了高家庄。高家庄有位高太公，他有三个女儿。大女儿和二女儿都已经嫁出去了，只剩下最小的女儿，名叫翠兰。高太公一直想为翠兰找个丈夫，留在家里干活。

这猪八戒见翠兰长得漂亮极了，便想要她做妻子。他把自己变成一个年轻人，去翠兰家，要见高太公。猪八戒对高太公说：

豬八戒原來是天上玉皇大帝的元帥，統領十萬天兵天將。可是有一次他在蟠桃會上喝醉了，調戲了仙女嫦娥，被趕出天界，到人間投胎。不幸的是，他投錯了胎，投到一隻大母豬的肚子裡去了，結果變成了一頭豬，所以姓豬，起名叫八戒。大家都叫他豬八戒。

豬八戒武藝高強，又懂得變身術。有一天他來到了高家莊。高家莊有位高太公，他有三個女兒。大女兒和二女兒都已經嫁出去了，只剩下最小的女兒，名叫翠蘭。高太公一直想為翠蘭找個丈夫，留在家裡幹活。

這豬八戒見翠蘭長得漂亮極了，便想要她做妻子。他把自己變成一個年輕人，去翠蘭家，要見高太公。豬八戒對高太公說：

"我姓猪，没有父母，也没有兄弟姐妹。我很会干活，不怕吃苦。我希望能跟翠兰结婚，做你的女婿，帮你下地干活。"高太公见这猪八戒长得又高又壮，看起来很会干活，便同意让他跟女儿结婚，做他的女婿，留在家里干活。

开始，猪八戒表现还不错，他下地耕田，收割粮食，样样都行。可是过了一年，猪八戒的模样慢慢变了；他的嘴巴越来越长，耳朵越来越大，饭也吃得越来越多，而且常常腾云驾雾，飞砂走石，把高太公一家和邻居都吓坏了。高太公这时候明白了，原来他给女儿找了个妖怪做丈夫。

于是，高太公到处去找法师来捉妖怪，要把猪八戒赶出去。猪八戒见高太公请法师来赶走自己，很生气。他把妻子关起来，不让她跟爸爸妈妈见面。高太公心焦如焚，因为请来的法师都不行，他们每次都被猪八戒打败了。

这天唐僧和徒弟孙悟空因为要往西天取经，路过高家庄。他们看见天黑了，就在高家庄住下来。晚上，孙悟空见村子里的人都很害怕，一个个哭哭啼啼的，就问他们为什么。他们说村子里有妖怪，这个妖怪会

"我姓豬，沒有父母，也沒有兄弟姐妹。我很會幹活，不怕吃苦。我希望能跟翠蘭結婚，做你的女婿，幫你下地幹活。"高太公見這豬八戒長得又高又壯，看起來很會幹活，便同意讓他跟女兒結婚，做他的女婿，留在家裡幹活。

開始，豬八戒表現還不錯，他下地耕田，收割糧食，樣樣都行。可是過了一年，豬八戒的模樣慢慢變了；他的嘴巴越來越長，耳朵越來越大，飯也吃得越來越多，而且常常騰雲駕霧，飛砂走石，把高太公一家和鄰居都嚇壞了。高太公這時候明白了，原來他給女兒找了個妖怪做丈夫。

於是，高太公到處去找法師來捉妖怪，要把豬八戒趕出去。豬八戒見高太公請法師來趕走自己，很生氣。他把妻子關起來，不讓她跟爸爸媽媽見面。高太公心焦如焚，因為請來的法師都不行，他們每次都被豬八戒打敗了。

這天唐僧和徒弟孫悟空因為要往西天取經，路過高家莊。他們看見天黑了，就在高家莊住下來。晚上，孫悟空見村子裡的人都很害怕，一個個哭哭啼啼的，就問他們為什麼。他們說村子裡有妖怪，

猪八戒变成
一阵风跑了

吃人，还把高太公的女儿关起来了。孙悟空说，"大家不要怕！我最会捉妖怪。"

一说完，孙悟空就来到了高太公家，到后院把翠兰放出来，然后自己变成翠兰的模样，守在房间里。没过多久，屋外狂风大作，原来是猪八戒回来了。变成翠兰模样的孙悟空故意叹口气说："今天我听我爸爸在外面骂你，还说请了一个法师来捉你。"猪八戒不以为意地说："不怕，不怕！谁都捉不到我。咱们上床睡觉吧！"孙悟空又说："我爸爸请的是龙宫借宝的孙悟空，你也不怕吗？"猪八戒一听，就吓得赶快往外跑。

孙悟空立刻现出原形，要捉猪八戒。猪八戒一见到孙悟空，就"呼"的一声，变成一阵风跑了。孙悟空跟着这阵风，紧紧地追赶着。它到哪儿，孙悟空就追到哪儿。最后這個妖怪會吃人，還把高太公的女兒關起來了。孫悟空說，"大家不要怕！我最會捉妖怪。"

　　一說完，孫悟空就來到了高太公家，到後院把翠蘭放出來，然後自己變成翠蘭的模樣，守在房間裡。沒過多久，屋外狂風大作，原來是豬八戒回來了。變成翠蘭模樣的孫悟空故意嘆口氣說："今天我聽我爸爸在外面罵你，還說請了一個法師來捉你。"豬八戒不以為意地說："不怕，不怕！誰都捉不到我。咱們上床睡覺吧！"孫悟空又說："我爸爸請的是龍宮借寶的孫悟空，你也不怕嗎？"豬八戒一聽，就嚇得趕快往外跑。

　　孫悟空立刻現出原形，要捉豬八戒。豬八戒一見到孫悟空，就"呼"的他们到了一座大山上，孙悟空拿出龙宫借来的宝器，对着猪八戒打过去，只几个来回，就把猪八戒打败了。

猪八戒被孙悟空打败以后，没有办法，只好做他的师弟，跟他一起保护唐僧去西天取经。猪八戒虽然好吃懒做，爱占小便宜，贪图女色，但是憨厚单纯，力气大，对师兄言听计从，对师父又忠心耿耿。猪八戒从此便成为孙悟空的好帮手，为唐僧去西天取经立下了汗马功劳。

一聲，變成一陣風跑了。孫悟空跟著這陣風，緊緊地追趕著。它到哪兒，孫悟空就追到哪兒。最後他們到了一座大山上，孫悟空拿出龍宮借來的寶器，對著豬八戒打過去，只幾個來回，就把豬八戒打敗了。

豬八戒被孫悟空打敗以後，沒有辦法，只好做他的師弟，跟他一起保護唐僧去西天取經。豬八戒雖然好吃懶做，愛佔小便宜，貪圖女色，但是憨厚單純，力氣大，對師兄言聽計從，對師父又忠心耿耿。豬八戒從此便成為孫悟空的好幫手，為唐僧去西天取經立下了汗馬功勞。

Vocabulary List

猪八戒娶亲　zhu bajie takes a wife

	SIMPLIFIED CHARACTERS	TRADITIONAL CHARACTERS	PINYIN	PART OF SPEECH	ENGLISH DEFINITION
1	玉皇大帝	玉皇大帝	*Yù Huáng Dàdì*	pn.	Jade Emperor Yu
2	元帅	元帥	*yuánshuài*	n.	commander-in-chief
3	统领	統領	*tǒnglǐng*	v.	to command
4	蟠桃	蟠桃	*pántáo*	n.	flat peach
5	调戏	調戲	*tiáoxì*	v.	to take liberties with
6	天界	天界	*tiānjiè*	n.	boundary of heaven
7	投胎	投胎	*tóu tāi*	vo.	to reincarnate
8	母猪	母豬	*mǔzhū*	n.	sow
9	变身术	變身術	*biànshēn shù*	n.	the art of physical transformation
10	高家庄	高家莊	*Gāojiā zhuāng*	pn.	Gao village
11	高太公	高太公	*Gāo Tàigōng*	pn.	Great-grandfather Gao
12	翠兰	翠蘭	*Cuìlán*	pn.	(name of a person)
13	女婿	女婿	*nǚxù*	n.	son-in-law
14	耕田	耕田	*gēng tián*	vo.	to farm the land
15	收割	收割	*shōugē*	v.	to harvest

	SIMPLIFIED CHARACTERS	TRADITIONAL CHARACTERS	PINYIN	PART OF SPEECH	ENGLISH DEFINITION
16	模样	模樣	*múyàng*	n.	appearance, look
17	腾云驾雾	騰雲駕霧	*téngyún jiàwù*	expr.	to mount the clouds and ride the mist
18	飞砂走石	飛砂走石	*fēishā zǒushí*	expr.	to launch a sandstorm
19	妖怪	妖怪	*yāoguài*	n.	monster
20	法师	法師	*fǎshī*	n.	master
21	捉	捉	*zhuō*	v.	to catch, to capture
22	心焦如焚	心焦如焚	*xīnjiāo rúfén*	expr.	extremely anxious
23	唐僧	唐僧	*Táng Sēng*	pn.	Monk Tang
24	徒弟	徒弟	*túdì*	n.	disciple
25	孙悟空	孫悟空	*Sūn Wùkōng*	pn.	(name of the Monkey King)
26	西天取经	西天取經	*xītiān qǔjīng*	expr.	traveling to the West to obtain scriptures
27	哭哭啼啼	哭哭啼啼	*kūkū títí*	v.	to endlessly weep and wail
28	后院	後院	*hòuyuàn*	n.	backyard
29	守	守	*shǒu*	v.	to guard
30	狂风大作	狂風大作	*kuángfēng dàzuò*	expr.	a sudden fierce wind
31	故意	故意	*gùyì*	adv.	intentionally

	SIMPLIFIED CHARACTERS	TRADITIONAL CHARACTERS	PINYIN	PART OF SPEECH	ENGLISH DEFINITION
32	叹口气	嘆口氣	tàn kǒuqì	vo.	to sigh
33	不以为意	不以為意	bùyǐwéiyì	expr.	to pay no attention to
34	现出原形	現出原形	xiànchū yuánxíng	vo.	to show one's original form
35	追赶	追趕	zhuīgǎn	v.	to chase
36	宝器	寶器	bǎoqì	n.	treasure
37	保护	保護	bǎohù	v.	to protect
38	好吃懒做	好吃懶做	hàochī lǎnzuò	expr.	gluttonous and lazy
39	占小便宜	佔小便宜	zhàn xiǎo piányi	vo.	to gain a cheap advantage
40	贪图女色	貪圖女色	tāntú nǚsè	vo.	to seek a woman's charms
41	憨厚单纯	憨厚單純	hānhòu dānchún	adj.	simple and honest
42	师兄	師兄	shīxiōng	n.	senior fellow apprentice
43	言听计从	言聽計從	yántīng jìcóng	expr.	to always follow somebody's advice
44	忠心耿耿	忠心耿耿	zhōngxīn gěnggěng	adj.	loyal and devoted
45	帮手	幫手	bāngshǒu	n.	helper, assistant
46	汗马功劳	汗馬功勞	hànmǎ gōngláo	expr.	deeds of valor in battle

Questions

Zhu Bajie convinced Gao Taigong to allow him to marry Cuilan by saying that he was

A. commander-in-chief under the Jade Emperor.

B. a pig.

C. an immortal.

D. a man unafraid of hard work.

What happened to Zhu Bajie after he started working for Gao Taigong?

A. His nose grew longer and his voice grew deeper.

B. He began to lose his voracious appetite.

C. His mouth grew longer and his ears grew bigger.

D. All of the above.

When Zhu Bajie learned that Sun Wukong was after him, he

A. became frightened and ran away.

B. surrendered himself to Gao Taigong.

C. became frightened and hid.

D. laughed and taunted Sun Wukong.

4 How was Zhu Bajie caught after Gao Taigong discovered that he was a monster?

A. He was locked up by his wife.
B. He was defeated by Sun Wukong in battle.
C. He was lured into a cage by Sun Wukong.
D. He was lured out of hiding with a large feast.

5 Which of the following qualities is Zhu Bajie known for?

A. Gluttony and laziness.
B. Eagerness for women's attention.
C. Honesty, loyalty, and devotion.
D. All of the above.

DISCUSSION

1. 玉皇大帝的元帅是怎样变成猪八戒的?
   玉皇大帝的元帥是怎樣變成豬八戒的?

2. 高太公为什么要把猪八戒赶出去?
   高太公為什麼要把豬八戒趕出去?

3. Make a flowchart and describe Zhu Bajie's transformation from heavenly commander-in-chief to junior monk.

4. How do Zhu Bajie's flaws and strengths reflect the values and teachings of Buddhism, specifically those pertaining to who can attain enlightenment?

APPENDIX:
STORY ABSTRACTS IN ENGLISH

I: CLASSICAL CHINESE POEMS

1. MISSING MY HOMETOWN ON A TRANQUIL NIGHT

Li Bai describes a quiet night lying on a bed in a moonlit room. Separated from his family and far from his hometown, he is in low spirits. Looking out his window, he thinks he sees frost on the ground. He then looks up and sees the bright moon, which he realizes is shedding light over everything. Lowering his head again, he thinks of his hometown and is overcome with homesickness.

2. SPRING MORNING

Meng Haoran portrays a calm spring morning after a night storm, when he awakes to the sound of birds singing and wonders how many flowers had fallen during the storm.

3. LOVE SEEDS

Full of affection, Wang Wei writes, "The red beans grow in the south; in the spring, they begin to sprout. Please gather as many as you can, because they represent fond memories."

4. PITYING THE FARMERS

Li Shen writes, "At noon, the peasants are hoeing up weeds in the fields. Their sweat drips into the soil. How many of us realize that each and every grain of rice in our bowls comes from their hard toil?"

5. VISITING THE PLAIN OF TOMBS

Li Shangyin writes, "At dusk my heart is filled with sadness. I drive my carriage to the plain of ancient tombs. I watch the setting sun, glorious and magnificent, but sadly coming to an end."

II: FAMOUS PLACES AND HISTORICAL SITES

6. BEIJING, CHINA'S CAPITAL CITY

Beijing is the capital, as well as the political, economic, and cultural center, of China. Its numerous historic sites include Tiananmen

Square, the Great Wall, the Summer Palace, the Temple of Heaven, and the Forbidden City. The 2008 Summer Olympics were held in Beijing, and the opening ceremony featured thousands of magnificent fireworks and a gigantic Chinese painting portraying the origin and development of China throughout its history. The theme of the Beijing Olympics was "One World, One Dream," and the theme song was "You and Me," which conveyed the Olympic spirit of peace, harmony, and solidarity.

7. THE GREAT WALL OF CHINA

The Great Wall of China is a symbol of ancient Chinese civilization and a source of pride among Chinese people. It is also one of the Seven Wonders of the World. The Great Wall was originally built during the reign of Qin Shi Huang for military defense, but nearly all of what is visible today was rebuilt in the Ming Dynasty. The Badaling section, located seventy five kilometers north of Beijing, has attracted millions of visitors from around the world, including Richard Nixon, Bill Clinton, and Margaret Thatcher.

8. XI'AN'S TERRACOTTA WARRIORS AND HORSES

Xi'an was an important city in ancient China and the capital of eleven Chinese dynasties. It is famous throughout the world for the tomb of Qin Shi Huang, the first emperor of the Qin Dynasty (255–210 B.C.E.). So far, three underground vaults containing thousands of life-size terracotta warriors and horses have been unearthed and officially opened to the public. They have often been referred to as "the Eighth Wonder of the Ancient World." The three vaults are well preserved in three modern exhibits and attract millions of visitors each year.

9. DUNHUANG ROCK CAVES

Dunhuang is an ancient city in what is now northwestern Gansu Province. It is known for its rock caves and prehistoric paintings. Located on the Silk Road, Dunhuang was a gateway between Central Asia and China and is now a noted tourist attraction surrounded by high sand dunes. It is home to over fifty thousand square meters of mural paintings inside 552 rock caves, including the Mogao Caves, which were created between the fifth and thirteenth centuries. While the majority of the paintings depict various Buddhist figures with unique expressions, others depict real life in ancient times. The paintings are representative of ancient Chinese culture, but also reflect influences from Indian, Greco-Roman, and Iranian civilization. Dunhuang is another of China's wonders and one of the world's greatest treasures.

10. TIBET'S POTALA PALACE

The Potala Palace is located in Lhasa, capital of the Tibet Autonomous Region. Built in 1645 by the fifth Dalai Lama, who used it as his winter palace, the Potala Palace was the religious and political center of Tibet. It is composed of the White Palace and the Red Palace, the former of which was the Dalai Lama's living quarters, while the latter was for religious use. The building measures four hundred meters from east to west and three hundred and fifty meters from north to south, containing more than one thousand rooms, ten thousand shrines, and about two hundred thousand statues, with a total area of one hundred and thirty thousand square meters. The Red Palace also houses many religious treasures; the Potala figures are beautiful examples of advanced fourteenth century art and rare secular iconography. Today, the Potala Palace, one of the largest architectural wonders of the world, functions as a museum.

III: LOVE STORIES

11. GIVING ONE'S BEST IN A TIME OF HARDSHIP

Once upon a time, two loving fish lived happily and peacefully in a river. One summer, it hardly rained, and the rivers dried up. These two fish were very worried and realized that they had to find a new home immediately, otherwise they would perish. They started to swim down the river, but the more they swam, the less water there was. Finally, they were stranded and could find no way back. By the third day, there was no more water. They gave each other the last bit of saliva in each of their mouths and died in a tight embrace that could not be torn apart.

12. THE DEER LOOKS BACK

A long time ago, there was a young man named Ah Hei who was poor and lived with his mother in a mountain village. One day,

Ah Hei went hunting and saw a beautiful deer being chased by a leopard. Ah Hei shot the leopard to save the deer. However, the deer kept running, and Ah Hei chased after her. After nine days and nine nights, they came to a cliff at the seaside where the deer had nowhere to go. Ah Hei could not bear to shoot, and the deer turned her head and looked back at Ah Hei. All of a sudden, the deer transformed into a beautiful girl. They fell in love instantly, got married, and lived happily ever after.

13. A BROKEN MIRROR REPAIRS ITSELF

In ancient China, there was a small state called Chen, where the king's sister was happily married to a man by the name of Xu. He foresaw a war approaching and was worried that he and his wife might be separated. Xu thus broke a mirror into two halves and gave one half to his wife, telling her to keep it as a symbol of their reunion. War broke out, and Xu's wife was taken away by the enemy. He traveled a long distance looking for his wife, and one day he saw an old servant selling half of a mirror in the market. He believed that the mirror belonged to his wife. Finally, they found each other and lived happily ever after.

14. THE CONQUEROR BIDS FAREWELL
TO HIS FAVORITE CONCUBINE

After the death of China's first emperor, Qin Shi Huang, the struggle for sovereignty came down to a conflict between Xiang Yu (232–202 B.C.E.), known as the Conqueror of Western Chu, and his rival. In the end, many of Xiang Yu's followers deserted him. One night, surrounded by enemy forces and low on supplies, he was sitting in his tent with his favorite concubine, Lady Yu, when he heard the sound of songs from Chu, his own homeland, coming from the attackers. Overwhelmed with sadness, Xiang Yu sat up late into the night singing a melancholy song over and over to Lady Yu. It is said that Lady Yu understood his sadness, and performed her last sword dance for him before taking her own life. Surrounded by attackers, Xiang Yu took his own life as well. This tragic love story has become legend and fascinated many Chinese people ever since.

IV: KNIGHT-ERRANT STORIES

15. SLEEPING ON FIREWOOD AND TASTING GALL

During the Spring and Autumn period (770–476 B.C.E.), the state of Wu (吴国 / 吳國) and the state of Yue (越国 / 越國) were constantly at war. During one of their battles, Wu defeated Yue and captured its king, Gou Jian (勾践 / 勾踐). The King of Wu, Fu Chai (夫差), took Gou Jian prisoner and had him raise horses. Gou Jian pretended to be loyal to Fu Chai, but never forgot about taking revenge. Many years later, Gou Jian was set free and returned to Yue. In order to make himself tougher, he worked in the fields with his subjects during the day, and tasted pig gallbladder and slept on firewood at night. A few years later, his country became strong and seized upon an opportunity to wipe out the state of Wu. This story has since been used to describe a person who endures self-imposed hardships to realize his or her ambition.

16. SCRAPING THE POISONED BONE FOR TREATMENT

Guan Gong (160–219 C.E.) was a general and a legendary hero who lived during the late Eastern Han dynasty and Three Kingdoms period. During a siege, Guan Gong was struck in the right arm by a poisonous arrow. The arrow was promptly removed, but the poison that was smeared on the arrowhead seeped deep into the bone. As he was unwilling to abandon the offensive campaign, his subjects had to send for the famed physician Hua Tuo to treat him. After examining the wound, Hua Tuo told Guan Gong that he had to cut open the flesh and scrape off the residual poison on the surface of the bone. In the absence of anesthesia, he also asked to tie up Guan Gong's injured arm to prevent movement. However, Guan Gong requested him to perform the surgery on the spot. Those around him cringed at the sound of the knife scraping the bone, but Guan Gong ate and drank, talked and laughed, and played chess as if he did not feel any pain, presumably to avoid damaging the morale of his army. This story of Guan Gong's bravery has since awed many people.

17. MU GUIYING, THE COMMANDER-IN-CHIEF

During the Song dynasty (960–1279), China was in a protracted war with invading armies from the north. In the Song army, there was a family of generals named the Yangs who fought victoriously in many battles against the invaders. But over time, the Yang army suffered tremendous losses; most of the male generals lost their lives, and those who were left were either girls or widows, known as the Women Generals of the Yang Family (杨门女将 / 楊門女將). These women were headed by Lady Mu Guiying, who grew up in a fortified mountain village and had acquired a good command of martial arts before she married into the Yang family. With the shortage of male generals, Mu Guiying took command and led the Yang army to victory against the invaders. She is one of the most celebrated women in the history of China. Chinese people remember her as a great female warrior who defended the northern territory and did her very best to protect her people.

18. THE HEROINE FENG WANZHEN

During the Qing dynasty, British-French allied forces attacked Beijing. Citizens of the city and its suburbs all rose in resistance. The village of Xie, located to the west of Beijing, was seriously threatened. The British and French were armed with rifles and cannons, while the Xie villagers only had swords and daggers. Under the leadership of nineteen-year-old Feng Wanzhen, the Xie villagers organized and prepared themselves for battle. Clad in dark uniforms, they ambushed the invaders and fought heroically. In the end, the villagers defeated the well-armed enemy troops and protected their home. Feng Wanzhen has since been praised for her bravery and wisdom and is widely respected as a heroine and model for young Chinese people, especially girls.

V: MYTHS AND FANTASIES

19. SHEN NONG TASTES HUNDREDS OF HERBS

Shen Nong (神农 / 神農), the Divine Farmer, was also known as the Yan Emperor (炎帝) and the Emperor of the Five Grains (五谷先帝 / 五穀先帝). A legendary ruler of China, he is a cultural hero of Chinese mythology believed to have taught agricultural practices, such as how to cultivate grains. He is said to have tasted hundreds of herbs to test their medicinal value, the basis on which he wrote a book entitled *The Divine Farmer's Herb-Root Classic*, 《神农本草经》/ 《神農本草經》. This work is considered the earliest Chinese pharmacopoeia; it includes 365 medicines derived from minerals, plants, and animals, and was crucial to the development of traditional Chinese medicine.

20. THE STORY OF EMPEROR SHUN

Shun Di (舜帝) was one of the five legendary emperors (五帝) of China between 2700 and 2200 B.C.E. Shun Di succeeded Emperor Yao (尧帝) at the age of fifty three and died at the age of one hundred, after relinquishing the seat of power to Yu the Great (大禹). Shun Di is believed to have ruled China for almost half a century, one of the longest reigns in Chinese history. In later centuries, Yao and Shun were glorified for their virtue. Shun was particularly renowned for his modesty and filial piety. According to legend, Shun was treated with hostility and jealousy by his stepmother and younger half-brother, yet he remained loving and free of resentment toward them. Thus, Emperor Yao gave Shun his daughter's hand in marriage and chose him as the successor. When Shun got old, he followed the example of Yao and passed his throne to Yu the Great.

21. LIN MONIANG, GODDESS OF THE SEA

Lin Moniang (960–987 C.E.) is widely worshipped as the Goddess of the Sea on the southeastern coast of China and neighboring areas. As the legend goes, she did not cry when she was born, so she was given the name 默娘, which means "Silent Girl." When she grew up, she was instilled with a divine power, with which she cured people of their diseases and rescued sailors from sea storms. It is said that she often wore red garments and stood on the shore to guide fishing boats home in the most dangerous and harsh weather. As a result, people were very grateful for her help and protection. They built temples to worship her, and they continue to revere her as the patron saint and protector of fishermen and sailors.

22. THE EIGHT IMMORTALS CROSS THE SEA

The Eight Immortals, the best-known group of immortals in Chinese mythology, consist of Han Zhongli (汉钟离 / 漢鐘離), Zhang Guolao (张果老 / 張果老), Tieguai Li (铁拐李 / 鐵拐李), Han Xiangzi (韩湘子 / 韓湘子), Cao Guojiu (曹国舅 / 曹國舅), Lü Dongbin (吕洞宾 / 呂洞賓), Lan Caihe (蓝采和 / 藍采和), and He Xiangu (何仙姑). Each were said to have a unique power, which could be transferred to a magical tool (法器) that could give life and destroy evil. One day, the Eight Immortals gathered to drink to their hearts' content. They each boasted of crossing the East Sea using his or her own powerful tool, and one by one, they crossed the surging sea.

23. ZHU BAJIE TAKES A WIFE

This story is part of the classical Chinese novel *Journey to the West*, (《西游记》 / 《西遊記》). It is a fictionalized account based on stories surrounding the Buddhist monk Tang Seng's pilgrimage to India to obtain Buddhist religious texts. It was a very dangerous journey, but Tang Seng made it with the help and protection of his three capable disciples: Sun Wukong, Zhu Bajie, and Sha Wujing. Zhu Bajie, the pig character in *Journey to the West*, was once an immortal who commanded one hundred thousand heavenly soldiers of the Milky Way. He was capable of thirty-six physical transformations and could travel on clouds. However, during a celebration of the gods, he drank too much and flirted with Chang E (嫦娥), the beautiful moon goddess. As a result, he was punished and exiled into the mortal world to be reborn as a human. As bad luck had it, he ended up in the womb of a sow, which turned him into a half-man, half-pig monster. His desire for women led him to Gao village, where he posed as a normal human being and took a wife. Later, when the villagers discovered that he was a monster, Zhu Bajie hid his wife away. At that point, Tang Seng and Sun Wukong were just passing through the village. After being captured by Sun Wukong, Zhu Bajie became a monk and joined Tang Seng's pilgrimage to the West.

VOCABULARY INDEX
生词索引
生詞索引

This vocabulary index is arranged in alphabetical order by *pinyin*. Homonyms appear in the order of their tonal pronunciation (i.e., first tones first, second tones second, third tones third, fourth tones fourth, and neutral tones last).

SIMPLIFIED CHARACTERS	TRADITIONAL CHARACTERS	PINYIN	PART OF SPEECH	ENGLISH DEFINITION	STORY NUMBER
A					
爱护	愛護	*àihù*	v.	to take good care of, to cherish	20
安危	安危	*ānwēi*	n.	safety and danger	17
翱翔	翱翔	*áoxiáng*	v.	to soar, to hover	9
奥林匹克运动会	奧林匹克運動會	*Àolínpǐkè Yùndònghuì*	pn.	The Olympics	6
B					
八达岭	八達嶺	*Bādálǐng*	pn.	(name of a section of the Great Wall)	7
拔剑	拔劍	*bá jiàn*	vo.	to pull out a sword	14
霸王	霸王	*Bàwáng*	pn.	The Conquerer	14
帮手	幫手	*bāngshǒu*	n.	helper, assistant	23
绑	綁	*bǎng*	v.	to bind, to tie	16
(向)傍晚	(向)傍晚	*(xiàng) bàngwǎn*	adv.	at dusk	5

SIMPLIFIED CHARACTERS	TRADITIONAL CHARACTERS	PINYIN	PART OF SPEECH	ENGLISH DEFINITION	STORY NUMBER
包括	包括	bāokuò	v.	to include	7
保存	保存	bǎocún	v.	to preserve	7
保护	保護	bǎohù	v.	to protect	23
宝库	寶庫	bǎokù	n.	treasure trove	10
堡垒式	堡壘式	bǎolěishì	adj.	fortress-style	7
宝器	寶器	bǎoqì	n.	treasure	23
保卫	保衛	bǎowèi	v.	to defend	18
宝物	寶物	bǎowù	n.	treasure	22
报仇	報仇	bàochóu	v.	to revenge, to avenge	15
暴风雷雨	暴風雷雨	bàofēng léiyǔ	expr.	violent winds and thunderstorms	20
豹子	豹子	bàozi	n.	leopard	12
悲壮	悲壯	bēizhuàng	adj.	moving and tragic	14
被迫	被迫	bèipò	v.	to be forced	13
本领	本領	běnlǐng	n.	skill, ability	22
比喻	比喻	bǐyù	n./v.	metaphor; to metaphorize	11
壁画	壁畫	bìhuà	n.	mural paintings	9
边关	邊關	biānguān	n.	border station	17
鞭子	鞭子	biānzi	n.	whip	19

SIMPLIFIED CHARACTERS	TRADITIONAL CHARACTERS	PINYIN	PART OF SPEECH	ENGLISH DEFINITION	STORY NUMBER
不幸	不幸	*bùxìng*	adj.	unfortunate	20
不以为意	不以為意	*bùyǐwéiyì*	expr.	to pay no attention to	23

c

灿烂	燦爛	*cànlàn*	adj.	magnificent, splendid	5
曹国舅	曹國舅	*Cáo Guójiù*	pn.	(name of an immortal)	22
草药	草藥	*cǎoyào*	n.	herbs	19
侧身	側身	*cèshēn*	vo.	to lie on one's side	11
柴草	柴草	*cháicǎo*	n.	firewood	15
尝	嘗	*cháng*	v.	to try, to taste	15
长安街	長安街	*Cháng'ān Jiē*	pn.	Chang'an Avenue	6
长城	長城	*Chángchéng*	pn.	the Great Wall	7
长处	長處	*chángchù*	n.	strong points	18
尝试	嘗試	*chángshì*	v.	to attempt, to try	19
朝拜	朝拜	*cháobài*	v.	to worship	21
撤退	撤退	*chètuì*	v.	to retreat	14
沉默	沉默	*chénmò*	adj.	silent	21
沉思	沉思	*chénsī*	v.	to ponder	1
成功	成功	*chénggōng*	v.	to succeed	15

SIMPLIFIED CHARACTERS	TRADITIONAL CHARACTERS	PINYIN	PART OF SPEECH	ENGLISH DEFINITION	STORY NUMBER
成熟可靠	成熟可靠	chéngshú kěkào	adj.	mature and reliable	17
成语	成語	chéngyǔ	n.	idiom, phrase	11
吃苦耐劳	吃苦耐勞	chīkǔ nàiláo	expr.	to bear hardships and withstand hard work	15
迟疑	遲疑	chíyí	v.	to hesitate	12
持续	持續	chíxù	v.	to continue	17
持续不停	持續不停	chíxù bùtíng	v.	to continue without stopping	19
耻辱	恥辱	chǐrǔ	n.	shame	15
充满深情	充滿深情	chōngmǎn shēnqíng	vo.	to be full of deep love and emotion	12
崇拜	崇拜	chóngbài	v.	to worship	16
抽打	抽打	chōudǎ	v.	to lash, to whip	19
抽枝	抽枝	chōu zhī	vo.	to put forth buds	3
出征	出征	chūzhēng	v.	to go out to battle	17
锄禾	鋤禾	chú hé	vo.	to hoe up weeds in the fields	4
锄头	鋤頭	chútou	n.	hoe	4
处死	處死	chǔsǐ	v.	to be put to death	15
处于困境	處於困境	chǔyú kùnjìng	expr.	to be in a predicament	11

SIMPLIFIED CHARACTERS	TRADITIONAL CHARACTERS	PINYIN	PART OF SPEECH	ENGLISH DEFINITION	STORY NUMBER
传递	傳遞	chuándì	v.	to convey	6
传统	傳統	chuántǒng	n.	tradition	6
垂下	垂下	chuíxià	vc.	to hang down	15
唇	唇	chún	n.	lips	11
翠兰	翠蘭	Cuìlán	pn.	(name of a person)	23
存放	存放	cúnfàng	v.	to store	7
存在	存在	cúnzài	v.	to exist	11

D

SIMPLIFIED CHARACTERS	TRADITIONAL CHARACTERS	PINYIN	PART OF SPEECH	ENGLISH DEFINITION	STORY NUMBER
搭弓	搭弓	dā gōng	vo.	to put the arrow on the bow	12
打猎	打獵	dǎliè	v.	to hunt	9
打落	打落	dǎluò	vc.	to knock down	2
大炮	大炮	dàpào	n.	artillery	18
大势已去	大勢已去	dàshì yǐqù	expr.	the situation is hopeless	14
大显神通	大顯神通	dàxiǎn shéntōng	expr.	to show or display one's magical powers	22
大着胆子	大著膽子	dàzhe dǎnzi	vo.	to be brave	18
代表	代表	dàibiǎo	v.	to represent	6
带兵	帶兵	dài bīng	vo.	to lead the army	14

SIMPLIFIED CHARACTERS	TRADITIONAL CHARACTERS	PINYIN	PART OF SPEECH	ENGLISH DEFINITION	STORY NUMBER
带领	帶領	dàilǐng	v.	to lead	18
单身像	單身像	dānshēn xiàng	n.	statue of a single figure	9
当时	當時	dāngshí	adv.	at that time	8
当午	當午	dāngwǔ	n.	noon time	4
祷告	禱告	dǎogào	v.	to pray	21
稻	稻	dào	n.	rice, paddy	19
道术	道術	dàoshù	n.	Taoist arts	22
登	登	dēng	v.	to mount, to climb	5
等待时机	等待時機	děngdài shíjī	vo.	to wait for an opportunity	12
滴	滴	dī	v.	to drip	4
低头	低頭	dī tóu	vo.	to lower one's head	1
敌情	敵情	díqíng	n.	enemy activity	7
地球	地球	dìqiú	n.	the Earth	6
地位	地位	dìwèi	n.	status	8
电光一闪	電光一閃	diànguāng yīshǎn	expr.	a sudden flash of lightning	12
雕塑	雕塑	diāosù	n.	sculpture	10
顶峰	頂峰	dǐngfēng	n.	high point, pinnacle	8
动静	動靜	dòngjìng	n.	movement, activity	18

SIMPLIFIED CHARACTERS	TRADITIONAL CHARACTERS	PINYIN	PART OF SPEECH	ENGLISH DEFINITION	STORY NUMBER
豆子	豆子	dòuzi	n.	bean	19
毒箭	毒箭	dújiàn	n.	poisoned arrow	16
独特	獨特	dútè	adj.	unique	10
渡过	渡過	dùguò	v.	to cross	22
短处	短處	duǎnchù	n.	shortcomings	18
对岸	對岸	duì'àn	n.	the opposite shore	22
对手	對手	duìshǒu	n.	opponent, adversary	14
敦煌	敦煌	Dūnhuáng	pn.	(name of a place)	9

F

发明	發明	fāmíng	v.	to discover	19
发射	發射	fāshè	v.	to fire	18
发芽	發芽	fā yá	vo.	to sprout	3
发展	發展	fāzhǎn	n./v.	development; to develop	6
法力	法力	fǎli	n.	supernatural power	21
法力无边	法力無邊	fǎli wúbiān	expr.	boundless power	22
法师	法師	fǎshī	n.	master	23
法术	法術	fǎshù	n.	magic arts	21
翻过	翻過	fānguò	vc.	to climb over	12

SIMPLIFIED CHARACTERS	TRADITIONAL CHARACTERS	PINYIN	PART OF SPEECH	ENGLISH DEFINITION	STORY NUMBER
翻身	翻身	*fānshēn*	vo.	to turn over	11
方形	方形	*fāngxíng*	adj.	square	7
房梁	房梁	*fángliáng*	n.	roof truss	15
防御	防禦	*fángyù*	v.	to guard against	7
纺纱	紡紗	*fǎngshā*	vo.	to spin yarn	15
放火	放火	*fàng huǒ*	vo.	to set on fire	18
放弃	放棄	*fàngqì*	v.	to give up	18
放枪	放槍	*fàng qiāng*	vo.	to fire a gun	18
飞砂走石	飛砂走石	*fēishā zǒushí*	expr.	to launch a sandstorm	23
飞天	飛天	*fēitiān*	pn.	flying *apsaras* (Buddhist deities/devas)	9
分别	分別	*fēnbié*	adv.	respectively	22
分离	分離	*fēnlí*	v.	to separate	13
分散	分散	*fēnsàn*	v.	to distract	16
分享	分享	*fēnxiǎng*	v.	to share	14
分心	分心	*fēnxīn*	vo.	to divert one's attention	14
奋力	奮力	*fènlì*	vo.	to do all one can	11
封建王朝	封建王朝	*fēngjiàn wángcháo*	n.	feudal dynasties	7

SIMPLIFIED CHARACTERS	TRADITIONAL CHARACTERS	PINYIN	PART OF SPEECH	ENGLISH DEFINITION	STORY NUMBER
高价	高價	*gāojià*	n.	high price	13
高粱	高粱	*gāoliang*	n.	sorghum (a type of grain)	19
高尚	高尚	*gāoshàng*	adj.	noble	16
高太公	高太公	*Gāo Tàigōng*	pn.	Great-grandfather Gao	23
割开	割開	*gēkāi*	vc.	to cut open	16
根	根	*gēn*	n.	root	6
耕田	耕田	*gēngtián*	vo.	to farm the land	23
更加	更加	*gèngjiā*	adv.	more	20
宫殿式	宮殿式	*gōngdiàn shì*	adj.	palace-style	10
攻陷	攻陷	*gōngxiàn*	v.	to storm, to capture	13
公元	公元	*gōngyuán*	n.	the Common Era	10
公主	公主	*gōngzhǔ*	n.	princess	13
勾践	勾踐	*Gōu Jiàn*	pn.	(name of a person)	15
古埃及	古埃及	*Gǔ Āijí*	pn.	Ancient Egypt	8
古迹	古迹	*gǔjì*	n.	historic site	6
骨头	骨頭	*gǔtou*	n.	bone	16
古原	古原	*gǔyuán*	n.	the plain of ancient tombs	5
谷子	穀子	*gǔzi*	n.	millet	19

SIMPLIFIED CHARACTERS	TRADITIONAL CHARACTERS	PINYIN	PART OF SPEECH	ENGLISH DEFINITION	STORY NUMBER
故宫	故宮	Gùgōng	pn.	the Imperial Palace	6
故乡	故鄉	gùxiāng	n.	hometown	1
故意	故意	gùyì	adv.	intentionally	23
刮去	刮去	guāqù	vc.	to scrape off	16
挂帅	掛帥	guà shuài	vo.	to assume command/ leadership (of a large army)	17
拐杖	拐杖	guǎizhàng	n.	cane	22
棺材	棺材	guāncai	n.	coffin	8
关系	關係	guānxi	n.	relation, relationship	9
观音菩萨	觀音菩薩	Guānyīn Púsà	pn.	Bodhisattva Guanyin	10
管理	管理	guǎnlǐ	v.	to manage	17
光彩	光彩	guāngcǎi	n.	splendor	8
光辉	光輝	guānghuī	adj.	radiant, brilliant	5
规模	規模	guīmó	n.	scale, dimension	10
桂花	桂花	guìhuā	n.	osmanthus flower	17
果然	果然	guǒrán	adv.	as expected	18
过江	過江	guò jiāng	vo.	to cross the river	14

H

SIMPLIFIED CHARACTERS	TRADITIONAL CHARACTERS	PINYIN	PART OF SPEECH	ENGLISH DEFINITION	STORY NUMBER
海拔	海拔	*hǎibá*	n.	height above sea level	10
海上女神	海上女神	*Hǎishàng Nǔshén*	pn.	Goddess of the Sea	21
憨厚单纯	憨厚單純	*hānhòu dānchún*	adj.	simple and honest	23
韩湘子	韓湘子	*Hán Xiāngzǐ*	pn.	(name of an immortal)	22
汗马功劳	汗馬功勞	*hànmǎ gōngláo*	expr.	deeds of valor in battle	23
汉钟离	漢鍾離	*Hàn Zhōnglí*	pn.	(name of an immortal)	22
好吃懒做	好吃懶做	*hàochī lǎnzuò*	expr.	gluttonous and lazy	23
喝醉	喝醉	*hēzuì*	vc.	to be drunk	22
河北省	河北省	*Héběi Shěng*	pn.	Hebei Province	7
荷花	荷花	*héhuā*	n.	lotus	22
和平	和平	*hépíng*	n.	peace	6
何仙姑	何仙姑	*Hé Xiāngū*	pn.	(name of an immortal)	22
横贯	橫貫	*héngguàn*	v.	to cross, to traverse	7
红豆	紅豆	*hóngdòu*	n.	red bean	3
后母	後母	*hòumǔ*	n.	stepmother	20
后院	後院	*hòuyuàn*	n.	backyard	23

SIMPLIFIED CHARACTERS	TRADITIONAL CHARACTERS	PINYIN	PART OF SPEECH	ENGLISH DEFINITION	STORY NUMBER
花篮	花籃	*huālán*	n.	flower basket	22
花鹿	花鹿	*huālù*	n.	spotted deer	12
画卷	畫卷	*huàjuàn*	n.	picture scroll	6
华佗	華佗	*Huà Tuó*	pn.	(name of a person)	16
黄昏	黃昏	*huánghūn*	n.	dusk	5
挥挥手	揮揮手	*huīhuī shǒu*	vo.	to wave one's hand	22
毁	毀	*huǐ*	v.	to destroy	18
火辣辣	火辣辣	*huǒlàlà*	adj.	burning hot	11
获胜	獲勝	*huò shèng*	vo.	to gain victory, to win	14

J

基部	基部	*jībù*	n.	base	7
几乎	幾乎	*jīhū*	adv.	almost	16
激烈	激烈	*jīliè*	adj.	fierce	17
疾病	疾病	*jíbìng*	n.	disease	19
极其	極其	*jíqí*	adv.	extremely	6
集中	集中	*jízhōng*	v.	to focus, to centralize	6
继续	繼續	*jìxù*	v.	to continue	12
记载	記載	*jìzǎi*	n./v.	record; to record	7

SIMPLIFIED CHARACTERS	TRADITIONAL CHARACTERS	PINYIN	PART OF SPEECH	ENGLISH DEFINITION	STORY NUMBER
嘉峪关	嘉峪關	*Jiāyù Guān*	pn.	Jiayu Pass	7
嫁	嫁	*jià*	v.	(of a woman) to marry	17
尖刀	尖刀	*jiāndāo*	n.	sharp knife	16
坚固	堅固	*jiāngù*	adj.	firm, strong	7
坚决	堅決	*jiānjué*	adv.	firmly	16
减少	減少	*jiǎnshǎo*	v.	to reduce	14
间断	間斷	*jiànduàn*	v.	to stop (doing something continuously)	15
建造	建造	*jiànzào*	v.	to build, to construct	6
建筑	建築	*jiànzhù*	n.	building, architecture	6
建筑群	建築群	*jiànzhù qún*	n.	group of buildings	10
骄傲	驕傲	*jiāo'ào*	n.	pride	6
交给	交給	*jiāogěi*	vc.	to hand over	21
交流	交流	*jiāoliú*	v.	to exchange	10
较低	較低	*jiàodī*	adj.	lower	11
皆	皆	*jiē*	adv.	all, each and every	5
接替	接替	*jiētì*	v.	to succeed	20
结晶	結晶	*jiéjīng*	n.	result, crystallization	10
解除	解除	*jiěchú*	v.	to remove	17

SIMPLIFIED CHARACTERS	TRADITIONAL CHARACTERS	PINYIN	PART OF SPEECH	ENGLISH DEFINITION	STORY NUMBER
解决	解决	*jiějué*	v.	to solve	19
介意	介意	*jièyì*	v.	to mind	16
借助	借助	*jièzhù*	vc.	to draw support from	22
金属	金屬	*jīnshǔ*	n.	metal	10
金字塔	金字塔	*jīnzì tǎ*	n.	pyramid	8
紧追不舍	緊追不捨	*jǐnzhuī bùshě*	expr.	to chase closely	12
尽头	盡頭	*jìntóu*	n.	the end	5
尽微力救助	盡微力救助	*jìn wēilì jiùzhù*	expr.	to help with all one's might	11
京城	京城	*jīngchéng*	n.	capital city	17
精华	精華	*jīnghuá*	n.	essence	10
经济	經濟	*jīngjì*	n.	economy	6
经历	經歷	*jīnglì*	v.	to experience	14
精美	精美	*jīngměi*	adj.	elegant	10
精神	精神	*jīngshén*	n.	spirit	6
景点	景點	*jǐngdiǎn*	n.	scenic spot	6
井井有条	井井有條	*jǐngjǐng yǒutiáo*	expr.	in perfect order	17

镜子	鏡子	*jìngzi*	n.	mirror	13
居住	居住	*jūzhù*	v.	to reside	10
举头	舉頭	*jǔ tóu*	vo.	to lift one's head	1
举行	舉行	*jǔxíng*	v.	to take place	6
据说	據說	*jùshuō*	conj.	it is said	14
诀别	訣別	*juébié*	vo.	to bid farewell	14
决心	決心	*juéxīn*	n.	determination	21

K

开幕式	開幕式	*kāimùshi*	n.	opening ceremony	6
考虑	考慮	*kǎolǜ*	v.	to consider	17
靠近	靠近	*kàojìn*	vc.	to draw close	11
可惜	可惜	*kěxī*	adv.	unfortunately	5
克林顿总统	克林頓總統	*Kèlíndùn zǒngtǒng*	pn.	President Clinton	7
口号	口號	*kǒuhào*	n.	slogan	6
哭哭啼啼	哭哭啼啼	*kūkū títí*	v.	to endlessly weep and wail	23
哭泣	哭泣	*kūqì*	v.	to cry	13
狂风大作	狂風大作	*kuángfēng dàzuò*	expr.	a sudden fierce wind	23

SIMPLIFIED CHARACTERS	TRADITIONAL CHARACTERS	PINYIN	PART OF SPEECH	ENGLISH DEFINITION	STORY NUMBER
梦想	夢想	mèngxiǎng	n.	dream	6
迷路	迷路	mí lù	vo.	to lose one's way	20
米	米	mǐ	n.	meter	9
眠	眠	mián	v.	to sleep	2
面	面	miàn	mw.	(measure word for mirrors)	13
庙宇	廟宇	miàoyǔ	n.	temple	21
灭掉	滅掉	mièdiào	vc.	to wipe out	15
民族风格	民族風格	mínzú fēnggé	n.	folk style	9
命令	命令	mìnglìng	v.	to order	17
磨练	磨練	móliàn	v.	to temper oneself	15
莫高窟	莫高窟	Mògāo Kū	pn.	Mogao Caves	9
谋臣	謀臣	móuchén	n.	advisor, counselor	15
模样	模樣	múyàng	n.	appearance, look	23
母猪	母豬	mǔzhū	n.	sow	23
目的	目的	mùdì	n.	purpose	7
木雕	木雕	mùdiāo	n.	wooden sculpture	10

SIMPLIFIED CHARACTERS	TRADITIONAL CHARACTERS	PINYIN	PART OF SPEECH	ENGLISH DEFINITION	STORY NUMBER
N					
难过	難過	*nánguò*	adj.	sad, sorrowful	11
难以忍受	難以忍受	*nányǐrěnshòu*	expr.	hard to bear	16
内涵	內涵	*nèihán*	n.	connotation, intention	10
内蒙古	內蒙古	*Nèiměnggǔ*	pn.	Inner Mongolia	7
尼泊尔	尼泊爾	*Níbó'ěr*	pn.	Nepal	10
尼克松总统	尼克松總統	*Níkèsōng zǒngtǒng*	pn.	President Nixon	7
泥塑艺术	泥塑藝術	*nísù yìshù*	n.	art of clay sculpture	8
泥土	泥土	*nítǔ*	n.	soil	11
泥制彩塑	泥製彩塑	*nízhì cǎisù*	n.	colored clay sculpture	9
鸟巢	鳥巢	*niǎocháo*	n.	bird's nest	6
宁夏	寧夏	*Níngxià*	pn.	Ningxia (Autonomous Region)	7
农事	農事	*nóngshì*	n.	farming, agricultural practice	19
奴仆	奴僕	*núpú*	n.	servant	15
女婿	女婿	*nǚxù*	n.	son-in-law	23

SIMPLIFIED CHARACTERS	TRADITIONAL CHARACTERS	PINYIN	PART OF SPEECH	ENGLISH DEFINITION	STORY NUMBER
P					
拍板	拍板	pāibǎn	n.	clappers	22
排成方阵	排成方陣	páichéng fāngzhèn	vo.	to line up in a square formation	8
蟠桃	蟠桃	pántáo	n.	flat peach	23
抛进	抛進	pāojìn	vc.	to toss in	22
盆子	盆子	pénzi	n.	basin	16
皮肉	皮肉	píròu	n.	flesh	16
飘曳	飄曳	piāoyè	adj.	floating, fluttering	9
品质	品質	pǐnzhì	n.	quality	16
平安无事	平安無事	píng'ānwúshì	expr.	safe and sound	18
平原	平原	píngyuán	n.	field, plain	18
平整	平整	píngzhěng	adj.	neat, smooth	7
凭证	憑證	píngzhèng	n.	proof, evidence	13
仆人	僕人	púrén	n.	servant	13
普陀山	普陀山	Pǔtuó Shān	pn.	Mount Putuo	10
Q					
骑兵	騎兵	qíbīng	n.	cavalrymen	9
奇迹	奇蹟	qíjì	n.	miracle, wonder	7

SIMPLIFIED CHARACTERS	TRADITIONAL CHARACTERS	PINYIN	PART OF SPEECH	ENGLISH DEFINITION	STORY NUMBER
奇特	奇特	qítè	adj.	peculiar	17
起源	起源	qǐyuán	n.	origin	6
砌成	砌成	qìchéng	vc.	to build by laying stones	7
气息	氣息	qìxī	n.	breath, flavor	6
谦虚谨慎	謙虚謹慎	qiānxū jǐnshèn	adj.	modest and prudent	20
前夕	前夕	qiánxī	n.	eve	14
浅浅的	淺淺的	qiǎnqiǎn de	adj.	shallow	11
抢劫	搶劫	qiǎngjié	v.	to rob	18
抢救	搶救	qiǎngjiù	v.	to rescue, to rush to save	21
妾	妾	qiè	n.	concubine	14
侵犯	侵犯	qīnfàn	v.	to invade	17
亲切	親切	qīnqiè	adj.	cordial, kind	6
秦始皇	秦始皇	Qin Shǐ Huáng	pn.	the first emperor of the Qin dynasty	7
秦始皇陵	秦始皇陵	Qín Shǐ Huáng Ling	pn.	the tomb of Emperor Qin Shi Huang	8
清朝	清朝	Qīngcháo	pn.	Qing dynasty	18
轻易	輕易	qīngyì	adv.	easily	18

SIMPLIFIED CHARACTERS	TRADITIONAL CHARACTERS	PINYIN	PART OF SPEECH	ENGLISH DEFINITION	STORY NUMBER
情景	情景	qíngjǐng	n.	scene, sight	16
情思	情思	qíngsī	n.	fond memories, affection, thoughts of romantic love	3
驱(驾)	驅(駕)	qū(jià)	v.	to drive (a horse, car, cart, etc.)	5
全身披挂	全身披掛	quánshēn pīguà	expr.	to be covered in armor	17
群像	群像	qúnxiàng	n.	statue of a group	9

R

燃放	燃放	ránfàng	v.	to ignite	7
让给	讓給	rànggěi	v.	to offer	20
热烈	熱烈	rèliè	adj./adv.	enthusiastic, enthusiastically	20
人心涣散	人心渙散	rénxīn huànsàn	expr.	to lose the popular morale	14
忍受	忍受	rěnshòu	v.	to bear	15
任务	任務	rènwù	n.	task	17
扔下	扔下	rēngxià	vc.	to abandon	18
融合	融合	rónghé	v.	to merge, to mix together	10

SIMPLIFIED CHARACTERS	TRADITIONAL CHARACTERS	PINYIN	PART OF SPEECH	ENGLISH DEFINITION	STORY NUMBER
生长	生長	*shēngzhǎng*	v.	to grow	3
盛大	盛大	*shèngdà*	adj.	grand	6
圣人	聖人	*shèngrén*	n.	sage	16
诗	詩	*shī*	n.	poem	13
师兄	師兄	*shīxiōng*	n.	senior fellow apprentice	23
石刻	石刻	*shíkè*	n.	stone inscription	10
时刻	時刻	*shíkè*	n./adv.	moment; constantly	15
石窟	石窟	*shíkū*	n.	stone cave	9
时期	時期	*shíqī*	n.	time period	7
食物	食物	*shíwù*	n.	food	19
士兵	士兵	*shìbīng*	n.	soldier	14
释放	釋放	*shìfàng*	v.	to set free	15
世纪	世紀	*shìjì*	n.	century	10
世界	世界	*shìjiè*	n.	world	7
事务	事務	*shìwù*	n.	affairs, matters, work	20
事先	事先	*shìxiān*	adv.	beforehand	20
收割	收割	*shōugē*	v.	to harvest	23
守	守	*shǒu*	v.	to guard	23

SIMPLIFIED CHARACTERS	TRADITIONAL CHARACTERS	PINYIN	PART OF SPEECH	ENGLISH DEFINITION	STORY NUMBER
拴着	拴著	*shuān zhe*	v.	to tie	15
霜	霜	*shuāng*	n.	frost	1
水洼	水窪	*shuǐwā*	n.	puddle, pool	11
顺利	順利	*shùnlì*	adj.	smooth, successful	22
丝绸之路	絲綢之路	*Sīchóu zhī Lù*	pn.	the Silk Road	8
四面楚歌	四面楚歌	*sìmiàn chǔgē*	expr.	to be besieged on all sides	14
宋朝	宋朝	*Sòngcháo*	pn.	Song dynasty	17
随时	隨時	*suíshí*	adv.	at any time	13
孙悟空	孫悟空	*Sūn Wùkōng*	pn.	(name of the Monkey King)	23

T

SIMPLIFIED CHARACTERS	TRADITIONAL CHARACTERS	PINYIN	PART OF SPEECH	ENGLISH DEFINITION	STORY NUMBER
贪图女色	貪圖女色	*tāntú nǔsè*	n.	a woman's charms	23
叹口气	嘆口氣	*tàn kǒuqì*	vo.	to sigh	23
唐僧	唐僧	*Táng Sēng*	pn.	Monk Tang	23
逃脱	逃脫	*táotuō*	v.	to escape	20
逃走	逃走	*táozǒu*	vc.	to escape	13
腾云驾雾	騰雲駕霧	*téngyún jiàwù*	expr.	to mount the clouds and ride the mist	23

SIMPLIFIED CHARACTERS	TRADITIONAL CHARACTERS	PINYIN	PART OF SPEECH	ENGLISH DEFINITION	STORY NUMBER
提	提	tí	v.	to carry, to lift	21
啼鸟	啼鳥	tíniǎo	n.	singing birds	2
体现	體現	tǐxiàn	v.	to embody, to reflect	6
体育场	體育場	tǐyùchǎng	n.	stadium	6
天安门广场	天安門廣場	Tiān'ānmén Guǎngchǎng	pn.	Tiananmen Square	6
天界	天界	tiānjiè	n.	boundary of heaven	23
天亮	天亮	tiānliàng	n.	daybreak	2
天坛	天壇	Tiāntán	pn.	the Temple of Heaven	6
填	填	tián	v.	to fill up	20
田径	田徑	tiánjìng	n.	track and field	6
调戏	調戲	tiáoxì	v.	to take liberties with	23
铁	鐵	tiě	n.	iron	10
铁拐李	鐵拐李	Tiě Guǎilǐ	pn.	(name of an immortal)	22
铜	銅	tóng	n.	copper	10
统领	統領	tǒnglǐng	v.	to command	23
痛快	痛快	tòngkuai	adj.	pleasant	5
投进	投進	tóujìn	vc.	to throw in	22

SIMPLIFIED CHARACTERS	TRADITIONAL CHARACTERS	PINYIN	PART OF SPEECH	ENGLISH DEFINITION	STORY NUMBER
投胎	投胎	tóutāi	vo.	to reincarnate	23
徒弟	徒弟	túdì	n.	disciple	23
吐	吐	tǔ	v.	to spit	11
土木建筑	土木建築	tǔmù jiànzhù	n.	construction	10
团结	團結	tuánjié	v.	to unite, to rally	6
团长	團長	tuánzhǎng	n.	regimental commander	18
推辞	推辭	tuīcí	v.	to decline (an appointment or invitation)	17
推举	推舉	tuījǔ	v.	to choose	20
唾沫	唾沫	tuòmo	n.	saliva, spittle	11

W

SIMPLIFIED CHARACTERS	TRADITIONAL CHARACTERS	PINYIN	PART OF SPEECH	ENGLISH DEFINITION	STORY NUMBER
挖	挖	wā	v.	to dig	20
外形	外形	wàixíng	n.	external form, exterior	6
完整	完整	wánzhěng	adj.	entire, complete	19
威风凛凛	威風凜凜	wēifēnglǐnlǐn	adj.	majestic-looking, awe-inspiring	17
唯一	唯一	wéiyī	adj.	only	11
尾鳍	尾鰭	wěiqí	n.	tail fin	11
味道	味道	wèidào	n.	taste	19

SIMPLIFIED CHARACTERS	TRADITIONAL CHARACTERS	PINYIN	PART OF SPEECH	ENGLISH DEFINITION	STORY NUMBER
位置	位置	wèizhì	n.	place	16
位子	位子	wèizi	n.	place, seat	20
瘟疫	瘟疫	wēnyì	n.	plague, epidemic disease	19
闻	聞	wén	v.	to hear	2
文化	文化	wénhuà	n.	culture	6
文圣	文聖	Wénshèng	pn.	Sage of Culture	16
文献	文獻	wénxiàn	n.	document	7
稳当	穩當	wěndang	adj.	secure, stable	22
屋顶	屋頂	wūdǐng	n.	roof	20
乌江	烏江	Wū Jiāng	pn.	the Wu River	14
无比	無比	wúbǐ	adj.	unparalleled, matchless	5
吴国	吳國	Wúguó	pn.	state of Wu	15
无路可逃	無路可逃	wúlùkětáo	expr.	no way out	12
无论如何	無論如何	wúlùn rúhé	conj.	no matter what	14
无限	無限	wúxiàn	adj.	boundless	5
五谷粮食	五穀糧食	wǔgǔ liángshi	n.	the five grains (rice, two kinds of millet, wheat, and beans)	19

SIMPLIFIED CHARACTERS	TRADITIONAL CHARACTERS	PINYIN	PART OF SPEECH	ENGLISH DEFINITION	STORY NUMBER
下游	下游	*xiàyóu*	n.	lower reaches of a river	11
先后	先後	*xiānhòu*	adv.	one after another	7
衔住	衔住	*xiánzhù*	vc.	to hold in the mouth	11
显灵	顯靈	*xiǎn líng*	vo.	to make one's power or presence felt	21
现出原形	現出原形	*xiànchū yuánxíng*	vo.	to show the original form	23
相会	相會	*xiānghuì*	v.	to meet	6
乡民	鄉民	*xiāngmín*	n.	villager	21
香味	香味	*xiāngwèi*	n.	sweet smell, fragrance	17
项羽	項羽	*Xiàng Yǔ*	pn.	(name of a person)	14
象征	象徵	*xiàngzhēng*	n.	symbol, emblem	3
箫管	簫管	*xiāoguǎn*	n.	flute	22
晓	曉	*xiǎo*	n.	dawn	2
孝敬	孝敬	*xiàojing*	v.	to be filial and respectful (to one's elders)	20
谢庄	謝莊	*Xièzhuāng*	pn.	Xie village	18
心得	心得	*xīndé*	n.	knowledge gained, reflections	19
心焦如焚	心焦如焚	*xīnjiāo rúfén*	expr.	extremely anxious	23
心目	心目	*xīnmù*	n.	mind, point of view	16

SIMPLIFIED CHARACTERS	TRADITIONAL CHARACTERS	PINYIN	PART OF SPEECH	ENGLISH DEFINITION	STORY NUMBER
信任	信任	xìnrèn	n.	trust	15
信仰	信仰	xìnyǎng	n.	faith, belief	10
形态	形態	xíngtài	n.	form, shape	8
幸运地	幸運地	xìngyùn de	adv.	fortunately, luckily	20
性质	性質	xìngzhì	n.	nature, quality	19
修理	修理	xiūlǐ	v.	to repair	20
修筑	修築	xiūzhù	v.	to build, to construct	7
虚弱	虛弱	xūruò	adj.	weak, feeble	11
宣扬	宣揚	xuānyáng	v.	to promote, to propagate	20
悬崖	懸崖	xuányá	n.	steep cliff	12
雪亮	雪亮	xuěliàng	adj.	shiny	18
血	血	xuè	n.	blood	16
血丝	血絲	xuèsī	n.	blood stain	11
寻找	尋找	xúnzhǎo	v.	to look for	13
迅速	迅速	xùnsù	adv.	quickly, swiftly	7

Y

烟火	煙火	yānhuǒ	n.	smoke and fire	7
烟雾	煙霧	yānwù	n.	smoke and fog	12
研究	研究	yánjiū	v.	to study, to research	21

SIMPLIFIED CHARACTERS	TRADITIONAL CHARACTERS	PINYIN	PART OF SPEECH	ENGLISH DEFINITION	STORY NUMBER
医药之祖	醫藥之祖	yīyào zhīzǔ	n.	the forefather of medicine	19
颐和园	頤和園	Yíhéyuán	pn.	the Summer Palace	6
以便	以便	yǐbiàn	conj.	so that	21
以少胜多	以少勝多	yǐshǎo shèngduō	expr.	to defeat many with a few	14
意	意	yì	n.	mood	5
异常	異常	yìcháng	adj.	abnormal	16
异香	異香	yìxiāng	n.	rare fragrance	21
意志	意志	yìzhì	n.	will	15
引人注意	引人注意	yǐnrén zhùyì	adj.	attractive	6
印度	印度	Yìndù	pn.	India	9
印象	印象	yìnxiàng	n.	impression	20
影响	影響	yǐngxiǎng	n.	influence	22
拥护	擁護	yōnghù	v./n.	to support, to uphold; support	17
永不分离	永不分離	yǒngbùfēnlí	expr.	to never separate, to be together forever	11
勇敢无畏	勇敢無畏	yǒnggǎn wúwèi	adj.	courageous, fearless	16

SIMPLIFIED CHARACTERS	TRADITIONAL CHARACTERS	PINYIN	PART OF SPEECH	ENGLISH DEFINITION	STORY NUMBER
用尽	用盡	yòngjìn	vc.	to use up completely	11
忧虑	憂慮	yōulù	v.	to worry	11
游客	遊客	yóukè	n.	tourist	7
有功的	有功的	yǒugōng de	adj.	meritorious	20
有勇有谋	有勇有謀	yǒuyǒng yǒumóu	adj.	brave and resourceful	17
虞姬	虞姬	Yú Jī	pn.	Concubine Yu	14
玉板	玉板	yùbǎn	n.	jade clappers	22
玉皇大帝	玉皇大帝	Yù Huáng Dàdì	pn.	Jade Emperor Yu	23
寓意	寓意	yùyì	n.	implied meaning, message	6
元帅	元帥	yuánshuài	n.	commander-in-chief	23
怨恨	怨恨	yuànhèn	v.	to hate, to have a grudge against	20
约	約	yuē	adv.	approximately	7
越国	越國	Yuèguó	pn.	state of Yue	15

Z

杂草	雜草	zácǎo	n.	weeds	19
藏传佛教	藏傳佛教	Zàngchuán Fójiào	pn.	Tibetan Buddhism	10

SIMPLIFIED CHARACTERS	TRADITIONAL CHARACTERS	PINYIN	PART OF SPEECH	ENGLISH DEFINITION	STORY NUMBER
政治	政治	*zhèngzhì*	n.	politics	6
知名人士	知名人士	*zhīmíng rénshì*	n.	public figure	7
汁液	汁液	*zhīyè*	n.	juice	19
指挥部	指揮部	*zhǐhuībù*	n.	headquarters	7
纸驴	紙驢	*zhǐlǘ*	n.	paper donkey	22
指引	指引	*zhǐyǐn*	v.	to guide	21
制高点	制高點	*zhìgāodiǎn*	n.	commanding point	7
至今	至今	*zhìjīn*	adv.	so far, to this day	7
中华民族	中華民族	*Zhōnghuá mínzú*	n.	the Chinese nationality	7
终生	終生	*zhōngshēng*	n.	all one's life	21
忠心耿耿	忠心耿耿	*zhōngxīn gěnggěng*	adj.	loyal and devoted	23
种子	種子	*zhǒngzi*	n.	seeds	19
中毒	中毒	*zhòngdú*	vo.	to be poisoned	19
周围	周圍	*zhōuwéi*	n.	surroundings	18
猪胆	豬膽	*zhūdǎn*	n.	gallbladder (of a pig)	15
主楼	主樓	*zhǔ lóu*	n.	the main building	10

SIMPLIFIED CHARACTERS	TRADITIONAL CHARACTERS	PINYIN	PART OF SPEECH	ENGLISH DEFINITION	STORY NUMBER
主帅	主帥	zhǔshuài	n.	commander-in-chief	17
主题歌	主題歌	zhǔtígē	n.	theme song	6
注意力	注意力	zhùyìlì	n.	attention	16
柱子	柱子	zhùzi	n.	pillar	16
抓走	抓走	zhuāzǒu	vc.	to arrest, to catch	13
装满	裝滿	zhuāngmǎn	vc.	to completely fill	16
追赶	追趕	zhuīgǎn	v.	to chase	23
捉	捉	zhuō	v.	to catch, to capture	23
滋润	滋潤	zīrùn	v.	to moisten	11
紫禁城	紫禁城	Zǐjìnchéng	pn.	the Forbidden City	6
仔细	仔細	zǐxì	adv.	carefully	13
自卫团	自衛團	zìwèituán	n.	self-defense corps	18
宗教	宗教	zōngjiào	n.	religion	9

ANSWER KEY (READING COMPREHENSION)

Story 1
1. B
2. D
3. B

Story 2
1. D
2. B
3. C

Story 3
1. B
2. A
3. B

Story 4
1. B
2. D
3. D

Story 5
1. A
2. C
3. D

Story 6
1. C
2. D
3. C
4. B
5. A

Story 7
1. D
2. A
3. B

Story 8
1. C
2. D
3. B

Story 9
1. D
2. A
3. B

Story 10
1. C
2. D
3. B

Story 11
1. A
2. C
3. B
4. D
5. B

Story 12
1. B
2. C
3. D
4. A
5. B

Story 13
1. C
2. B
3. D

Story 14
1. A
2. D
3. B

Story 15
1. D
2. C
3. B

Story 16
1. A
2. D
3. A
4. B
5. C

Story 17
1. B
2. D
3. A

Story 18
1. C
2. B
3. C

Story 19
1. B
2. D
3. C
4. C
5. D

Story 20
1. A
2. D
3. C

Story 21
1. D
2. B
3. A

Story 22
1. B
2. C
3. A

Story 23
1. D
2. C
3. A
4. B
5. D

ABOUT THE AUTHORS

Yun Xiao is Professor of Chinese Language and Linguistics at Bryant University. She has a Ph.D. degree in linguistics. Her research interests are second language acquisition and pedagogy, Chinese syntax and discourse analysis, and Chinese teacher education. Her recent publications include more than twenty articles and book chapters. She is the primary author of *Tales and Traditions* (Volumes 1–4); and co-editor of *Teaching Chinese as a Foreign Language: Theories and Applications*.

Ying Zhang is currently a lecturer of Chinese as a second language at China University of Geosciences. She has over twelve years of second/foreign language teaching experience at the college and grade-school level. She has taught in many Chinese programs in the US, South Asia, and China. She obtained her B.A. in language education at Central China Normal University and her M.A. at Wuhan University. Her areas of interest are second language acquisition, instructional design, material development, and integrating technology into Chinese teaching, as well as teacher development.

Chunching Chang received her B.A. degree in Chinese language and literature from National Cheng Kung University, Taiwan, and her M.A. degree in Chinese language and literature from the University of Massachusetts Amherst. Her research interests are Chinese linguistics and pedagogy. She has taught Chinese as a second/foreign language at National Cheng Kung University in Taiwan and at the University of Massachusetts Amherst.